The Program

How a Con Man Survived the Federal Bureau of Prisons' Cult of RDAP

By Matthew B. Cox

cult (kuhlt) *noun*: **1** a system of devotion directed toward a particular figure or object, **2** a relatively small group of people having beliefs or practices regarded by others as strange or sinister, **3** a misplaced or excessive admiration for a particular person or thing.

The Program. Copyright 2020 by Matthew Bevan Cox.

All rights reserved. The scanning, uploading, and distribution of this book without permission is a theft of the author's property. If you would like permission to use material from the book (other than for a review purpose), please contact the author at: contact.matthew.cox@gmail.com. Thank you for your support of the author's rights.

Library of Congress Cataloging-in-Publication Data is available on file.

Cover design by Matthew B. Cox

Author photograph by Brittney A. Mingo

Printed in the United States of America

Prologue

"A cult is a cult ... they strip you of your personality and rebuild it in their image."—Bill Maher

A SINGLE BEAD OF PERSPIRATION slowly runs down my forehead. I sit rigidly, surrounded by one hundred and fifty federal inmates who would soon become my peers in the Bureau of Prisons' Residential Drug Abuse Program. My brethren.

Fourteen rows of inmates, ten to eleven men per row, packed tightly into a large mixed activity room within one of the prison's massive housing units. The seating is split into sections—each facing one another. All of them (including myself) wear serious faces and pressed prison issued hunter green uniforms with polished black boots.

The sweat drip trickles down my nose and the entire group abruptly stands to recite the program's philosophy.

In an emotionless monotone, all one hundred and fifty prisoners say, in unison, "I am committed to my treatment for the betterment of my life through community as a method. Humbly I present myself..." As the group—or "the community" as I will come to know it—simultaneously utters their credo the atmosphere takes on a cult-like air. "I will embrace my community with honesty, integrity, a genuine heart, and an open mind." In the other members faces I can see a combination of emotions ranging from indifference to true conviction, but buried behind it all I see fear. "Yesterday, I was the problem," they conclude, "tomorrow, I will be the solution." Goosebumps ripple across the skin of my arms.

THE RESIDENTIAL DRUG ABUSE PROGRAM (RDAP) is an intensive nine-month, 500-hour substance abuse rehabilitation program administered by the Federal Bureau of Prisons (BOP), offered to federal prisoners. Prisoner-participants are taught to identify patterns of thinking that lead to self-destructive actions and beliefs in order to improve their coping skills.

That's the antiseptic definition. Sounds benign and non-obtrusive, however, the program is anything but. The Residential Drug Abuse Program's name itself is misleading. In fact, the program has nearly nothing to do with drug abuse and everything to do with comprehensive behavior modification.

To achieve this, RDAP uses a therapeutic community model. First, they isolate the program-participants from the general prison population by placing them in a separate housing unit —a prison within a prison. There, the inmates experience living in a "pro-social community."

Second, much like George Orwell's novel *Nineteen Eighty Four*,* —wherein citizens are under constant surveillance by Big Brother, the Thought Police, and Party members—while in the pro-social community participants are relentlessly monitored by their fellow peers.

---

* *Nineteen Eighty-Four*, a dystopian novel written by George Orwell, published in June 1949, whose themes center on the risks of totalitarianism and repressive regimentation of all persons and behaviors within society. The novel is set in an imagined future, the year 1984, when much of the world has fallen victim to perpetual war and the omnipresent government surveillance.

Twenty-four hours a day, seven days a week, month, after month, after month there is always someone watching, ready to correct every infraction, and eager to inform the staff.

Third, all participants must attend daily group sessions attended by Drug Treatment Specialists (DTS) and occasionally the RDAP coordinator. These classes are designed to break the participants' dysfunctional psyches down, examine the causes of their damaged core, and create an individualized program to correct their behavior.

If I'm going to be honest with you, the overwhelming immersion in the community as well as the program is nothing short of emotionally exhausting.

Why prisoners subject themselves to such a psychologically brutal process is simple; upon completion, participants receive a one-year reduction in their sentence. However, that was not why I entered the program.

Chapter One

"Here's an easy way to figure out if you're in a cult: If you're wondering whether you're in a cult, the answer is yes."—Stephen Colbert

MY NAME IS MATTHEW B. COX and I'm a con man. I'd love to tell you that I'm the classic confidence man depicted in Hollywood films—young, tall, and strikingly attractive. However, I stand a mere five-foot six-inches and I'm only moderately handsome for a guy in his late-forties.

I'm presently serving a lengthy prison sentence for a variety of bank fraud related charges, and I'm one hundred percent guilty of them all.

During my tenure, according to federal law enforcement, my mortgage company was responsible for roughly $40 million in fraudulent mortgage loans. According to the U.S. prosecutors, I was personally guilty for an *additional* $15 million—give or take a million.

As if that's not bad enough, when the FBI attempted to arrest me, I fled. While on the run I bilked several banks out of a few more million—at the time it felt like the right thing to do. However, as a result of this, the Secret Service placed me at the head of their most wanted list.

There was a significant amount of media coverage—dozens of newspaper articles chronicling my crime spree as well as pieces in *Fortune*, *Bloomberg*, and *Forbes* magazines. In addition, CNBC's *American Greed* and *Dateline* did a couple slash and burn episodes on me. None of the stories were flattering, but most were true.

After three years of dogged pursuit by the FBI, Secret Service, and the U.S. Marshals, I was captured and sentenced to twenty-six years. Had it not been for the brilliance and compassion of an inmate named Frank Amodeo, I would have done every day of that time. Fortunately, over the course of several years and multiple filings, Amodeo chipped away at my sentence; eventually getting my time reduced by twelve years.

Currently, I'm incarcerated at the Coleman Federal Correctional Complex in Central Florida. Coleman is a massive facility encompassing five distinct prisons. I'm housed at the low security prison, which holds approximately 2,000 inmates, interned within twelve housing units. It's not a bad place, as prisons go. Plus, it's located less than a one hour drive from my mother's house. That's the issue.

My mother comes to see me every two weeks, religiously. She's come through her breast cancer treatments, my father's deterioration from Alzheimer's and his eventual death from lung cancer. She's a real trooper, however, she's also eighty-eight-years-old and recently had a stroke. It's the consensus of my siblings that our mother lives for her visits with me. Unfortunately, the BOP has been pressuring my counselor to transfer me to the federal camp in Miami. If that happens, my fear is I'll never see her again.

"What about the FREE Program?" I ask my buddy Pierre Rausini over lunch. Pete was convicted of murdering two federal informants—I know how it sounds, but he's a super nice guy. I was desperate to find a way to get the BOP to place what's known as a "management variable" on me. Specifically, the designation restricts an inmate's movement to one prison.

"Nope," Pete replies, shaking his freshly shaved head, "I checked, the next one doesn't start for six months. You'll be gone by then." A sure way to obtain a management variable is by entering one of the bureau's special programs. "It's RDAP or you're shipped."

"I can't do it." I'd heard horror stories about the program for ten years. Fraudsters and con men didn't do well. "I'll never pass—"

"You don't have to pass. You only have to stay long enough to get the management variable placed on you, then you can dropout."

That's how I ended up sitting in what's known as the "morning meeting" in the RDAP-Housing Unit on June 15, 2017.

THE RDAP COORDINATOR, Dr. Michelle Smith,* stepped into the room. Sheathed in black slacks and a blouse with a long sheer scarf, her long straight, raven hair and slender physique give her a Morticia Adams** bewitchment. All eyes are on her—she alone holds the authority to make or break the participants' treatment. More specifically, with the stroke of a pen she can cut a year's incarceration off the prisoners' sentences and recommend an additional year of halfway house; and she wields this power like a fickle third world dictator.

* First name has been changed.
** The Addams Family, a satirical TV series in the mid 1960's depicting an oddly wealthy aristocratic clan who delight in the macabre.

Even the staff monitoring the morning meeting stiffen at her attendance. There are five of them, Drug Treatment Specialists (DTS), which facilitate the various groups through each phase of the program. All of them attend the morning meetings. All dance to the beat of The Doctor's drum.

"The community is sick," announces Dr. Smith. She is visibly irritated with the group of inmates. "You guys complain that I treat you like children, but you can't follow the simplest rules." The Doctor drones on and on.

I turn to the prisoner seated beside me—Robert Jackson,*** a phase one peer like myself—and whisper something about the insanity. Jackson immediately informs me that he refuses to take part "in this government-sponsored good citizen indoctrination program. I will *not* be brainwashed by these people. They can keep that fucking year." I quickly realize that Jackson is in serious need of psych-meds. He informs me he's "signing out of the program right after this absurdity ends." At that moment I catch Dr.

Smith stating, "I have a PhD."

*** Robert Blake Jackson was sentenced to 3 years in federal prison for making false statements in a federal investigation. In October 2014, Jackson's posted comments on his Facebook account expressing support for extremist terrorist groups such as ISIS. When questioned by the FBI he denied he'd posted the material.

A minute later she says it again. By the time Morticia sashays out of the meeting I've counted four separate instances where she's interjected her PhD into her lecture. I can't help but wonder, *What's she compensating for?*

Sure enough, an hour after the meeting, an agitated Robert Jackson stomps into Dr. Smith's office like a raging bull; he demands she remove him from the program and transfer him back to his old housing unit. It's a voluntary program, so, signing him out shouldn't be an issue. Still, I've heard rumors of The Doctor's uncanny ability to manipulate the inmates, but Jackson is headstrong. *No way she's changing his mind*, I tell myself. *That dude's outta here for sure.*

Ten minutes later, Jackson meekly steps out of Dr. Smith's office holding a rubber ball. As he approaches me I ask, "You outta here?" and he replies, "I wasn't thinking clearly. She gave me a stress ball." Squeezing the sphere furiously. He continues, "I'm staying."

Hands down, Dr. Smith is one of the most manipulative individuals I have *ever* encountered.

ANOTHER ISSUE WITH ENROLLING in the program is FRP (Financial Responsibility Program). Those inmates that owe fines or restitution are required to make monthly FRP payments. If an inmate refuses to pay or cannot pay, he or she is placed on FRP "refusal" status and his or her privileges are severely curtailed. The restrictions range from being banned from purchasing commissary to the loss of inmate employment. Unfortunately, I have $6 million in unpaid restitution, therefore, I am required to pay FRP. However, I've managed not to make one FRP payment while remaining off of refusal status for over a decade.

I managed to do this by taking advantage of the inefficiency of the BOP's staff. Within days of arriving at the Coleman Complex, I met with my Counselor, Karen Bates.* She went over several of the institution's rules, then pointed out that I had a hefty restitution. "Next month you're gonna have to start making FRP payments."

_{* First name has been changed.}

I'd just been given a twenty-six year sentence. My projected release date, with time off for good behavior, was 2030 and they wanted me to work the entire time for slave wages to pay back the money. I know this is going to sound unrepentant, but my first thought was, *Fuck that!* "I don't think so," I responded. "I specifically recall my lawyer convincing the judge to put off my payments until I'm released." This was an absolute lie; however, I figured the worst that would happen was she'd call my bluff. "You can check the file."

She looked at my file, which was around two inches thick and said, "I've never seen a Judgement and Commitment that doesn't require payments, but I'll check it out and get back with you later this week."

She didn't call me back within the week or the following week. Four months went by and Counselor Bates died in her sleep—she smoked three packs a day and had some health issues.

During my six month "team"—a review of an inmate's rehabilitation attended by the prisoner's counselor as well as their case manager and unit manager—I was asked by my new counselor, "Why aren't you paying FRP?"

"I don't have to," I replied. I then told them the same story I'd told Counselor Bates, six months earlier. "You can check my Judgement and Commitment."

"Oh, I will. Trust me I'll take a look," said my counselor, but he didn't check. Nor did my next case manager or the next one.

During one team, I acted so indignant at the fact that I was being questioned regarding my lack of FRP payments, I convinced my case manager to make a note in the system. The memo attested that my Judgement and Commitment stated that I wasn't required to take part in the FRP program.

Due to the laziness of the staff and despite the fact that my Judgement and Commitment clearly states that I am required to participate in the program, I have never made one FRP payment, nor have I ever been placed on refusal status.

Herein lies the issue, I know that the RDAP staff will thoroughly review my file. At that point, my little con will be revealed.

"I'm amazed that you got away with it for this long," says Pete, when I tell him. "They are definitely going to catch it."

"Damn," I grunt. "I was really hoping to go the distance."

CONTENT GROUP ISN'T EXACTLY the torturous Ludovico rehabilitation therapy depicted in *A Clockwork Orange*, * but it ain't far removed. Sitting in a semi-circle listening to twenty-plus inmates complaining for two hours certainly feels like torture.

* The 1971 film *A Clockwork Orange* chronicles the horrific crime spree of Alex (played by Malcolm McDowell) and his gang of juvenile delinquents, his capture, and attempted rehabilitation via an experimental psychological conditioning technique (the "Ludovico Technique").

My group includes Jackson as well as Shannon Ashworth, a tatted-up career-criminal methamphetamine-trafficker, nearly two dozen other guys, and a hulk of a black guy named William Duff. Most of the participants are mid-level drug dealers. All of them are here for the year off.

Our DTS is a white woman in her late fifties with a short boy's haircut who has a habit of speaking to the inmates like they're children. Karin DeMille ** seems nice; however, I know she's prone to extreme mood swings. Bipolar is a term often used to describe her. Everyone is concerned with staying on her good side.

** Name has been changed from NeSmith to DeMille, specifically to remove confusion—there are multiple characters within the story with some version of Smith within their name.

During our first session DeMille discusses the program material—seven softcover elementary school booklets designed to help us on our "journey to recovery." She then asks us to identify our "thinking errors and how they led to your being involved in illegal activities."

Some of the guys point to their addiction, but most of them blame their incarceration on the "snitch" in their cases. Few are willing to take direct responsibility. I, on the other hand, am not motivated to downplay my crimes or shift blame. Therefore, when it's my turn I admit to being selfish and antisocial. "I lack concern for how my actions affect others."

DeMille seems shocked by my answer as do my fellow peers. "Yes," she presses, "but why?"

"I'm narcissistic." I've known this about myself for a long time, I tell her, but knowing it hasn't helped me alter the behavior.

"Yes, but why?" she asks again. I reply DNA and she retorts, "But why, Mr. Cox, why?" I glance around the room at blank faces. I'm confused by her question as is everyone else. DeMille seems to be enjoying my uncertainty and she repeats the question, "Why Mr. Cox, why?"

I lean forward and say, "I'm not a psychiatrist. I don't know the specific genetic or environmental reason." DeMille huffs in irritation. She reiterates the question and I decide to draw a line in the sand. "Lady," I snap, "I've got a firm grasp of the English language, so, if I'm not understanding your question it's because I'm being given *poor* instructions!"

DeMille never challenges me again. In fact, because I pushed back, she becomes one of my biggest supporters.

AS A NEW PEER I'm constantly being bombarded by the seasoned RDAP members—guys that have been thoroughly indoctrinated into the program and are ready to spout propaganda on command. "Hi," they say, "my name's Mr. Laist, welcome to RDAP. If you need anything I'm in cell one-ten."

My first day in the unit I'm approached nearly ten times.

"It's fuckin' bizarre," I tell Pete at dinner. "It's like they've been brainwashed. They're like automatons." He chuckles at this.

"It's not funny, bro, I've watched five guys try and sign out of the program and Dr. Smith talks them out of it within minutes... I'm fuckin' terrified of that chick."

"It's only a couple months."

The following day, June 29, 2017, I'm sitting in my process DTS's office answering question for my "psycho-social." It's a diagnostic test used to help the DTS design a treatment plan specific to your needs. After DTS Garcia finishes questioning me about my childhood, addiction, and crimes, he asks, "Is there anything you hope to get out of the program; issues you'd like to address?"

I almost say, no, but then I think, *Fuck it. I'll throw him a bone.* "Yeah, you know if we could work on the narcissism, you know, tone it down to the point where I could focus on other people when they're talking, that would be great."

"What's happening when they're talking now?"

"Now?" I scoff. "Now, the whole time someone else is talking, I'm searching for an opportunity to talk about myself." He appears astonished. "It's so bad," I continue, "I've walked away from conversations and I couldn't tell you what we'd talked about. I'd just like to genuinely care about another person, you know? Or at least care enough to fake it."

Garcia mouth opens slightly and I almost laugh.

SOME INMATES DO THEIR TIME in the recreation yard. Others learn to play an instrument. I spend my time in the institution's library writing my fellow inmates' true crime stories. It probably sounds strange, but I've managed to get several of my subjects into Rolling Stone magazine, published several books, and even optioned the film rights to a few of my stories. Not bad for a guy in prison.

I've collected over a dozen true crime synopses—which I hope to sell the film rights to upon my release—and I'm in the process of writing another half a dozen.

My current issue, however, is the constant classes, committees, meetings, workshops, and special assignments; they make it very difficult for me to find the time to write. The workload, although it's not difficult, is time-consuming.

I've got an approximate idea of when the management variable will be placed on me, but there's no guarantee. Until I know it's been placed on me, have to participate in not only the daily morning meetings, content and process groups, but also the biweekly Alcoholics Anonymous meetings and multiple workshops.

They're a real pain, so, I make a point of taking The Doctor's clerk aside—an inmate named Cristian Tamayo. * After a quick chitchat, I learn that none of the staff verify our participation sheets. Therefore, I never go to my required AA meetings and, after a couple of workshops, I've got the signatures of the instructors down; so, I stop going to those classes as well.

* Cristian Tamayo was convicted of conspiracy to kidnap on February 27, 2012, and, eventually, he was sentenced to 101 months.

Shortly thereafter, my group is required to complete daily RSA (Rational Self Analysis) reports. However, I quickly realize that Dr. Smith only periodically checks whether the participants are actually doing their reports. This is done by collecting the last ten RSA's. So, to circumvent this exercise, I begin writing out the same ten RSA's every ten days.

The combination of these little tricks free up a couple hours in my day so I can continue working.

"DOES ANYONE HAVE A PULL-UP?" asks the inmate-facilitating the morning meeting. Understand, part of the program focuses on "accountability." Participants are required to "hold their peers accountable" for their actions—even the most minor of infractions are grounds for what's called a "pull-up."

Several hands shoot into the air and the facilitator points to a chunky inmate named Brad Mingo, * who stands. According to the format, he states his name, group, and the phase he's currently in. "I'd like to address Mr. Johnson," he says. ** Johnson apprehensively stands. Mingo then proceeds to explain that he, Johnson, and a third peer, as well as a non-RDAP-inmate, were having lunch in the cafeteria when the inmate asked if anyone wanted salt for their chicken.

Keep in mind, prisoners are prohibited from bringing condiments into the cafeteria—a rule that almost no one follows, however, RDAP participants are required to follow *all* of the rules.

* Name has been changed.
** Name has been changed.

"You know we aren't allowed to use that salt, but you took it anyway," said Mingo. "You're struggling with Super Optimism, Discontinuity, and Cut Off?"

Unexpectedly, DTS DeMille interrupts. She looks around the room at the one hundred and fifty inmates and asks who the third peer at the table was. The third peer immediately stands and barks out his name, group, and phase. "I saw the whole thing," he admits.

"I didn't see your hand raised," snaps DeMille. "Why didn't you pull-up Mr. Johnson?"

Panicked, he explains that he'd spoken with two senior peers and "both said it wasn't worth addressing."

This sent DeMille into a state of agitation. "Not important?! Who were the other peers you spoke with?" He then pointed them out and they stood. "You don't think breaking the rules is important?" Exasperated, she looks around the room in a manic state and scoffs, "Two *senior* peers think that breaking the rules *isn't* important?!"

There were now five guys standing at attention in the morning meeting; four of which had their heads on the chopping block. In the midst of this silliness I turn to the peer sitting next to me and whisper, "Is all of this over salt?" He glances at me and nervously shakes his head, indicating not to talk to him. He looks terrified.

Dr. Smith closes out the meeting with a lecture on seemingly unimportant decisions or SUDS. "These decisions can evolve into catastrophic thinking errors," she says. "Believe it or not, something as small as sneaking a piece of bread out of the cafeteria can lead to embezzling from an employer or worse."

That makes about as much sense, I tell myself, *as smoking cigarettes leads to shooting heroin.*

She saunters between the rows, looks over the sea of prisoners, and continues, "You don't know the complexities of the behavior modification or the therapeutic community model." She informs us that we're "just inmates. You don't understand your disease. I have a PhD." *Jesus Christ! Every time this chick talks she brings up her fuckin' degree.* "The community is sick, sick ... sick."

Three hours later, I'm sitting at lunch with Pete complaining about being locked up with the leader of Heaven's Gate—a UFO religious cult based in California.

"Relax." He grins. "They don't sell Nikes or jumpsuits at commissary." The cult was led by Marshal Applewhite, a Christian eschatologist New Age guru. Specifically, members were convinced by Applewhite that an extraterrestrial spacecraft was coming to take them to another planet; all they had to do was transcend their human shell. In March 1997, nearly forty cult members took their own lives in a mass suicide. All were wearing matching white Nikes and jumpsuits.

"I'm telling you Pete, she's brainwashing these guys."

At that moment, an RDAP peer, Michael Conover, * sits down at our table with his tray of square pizza. Pete, Mike, and myself had been mocking the insanity of RDAP two weeks earlier. So, I'm not worried when Pete turns to him and says, "How about you Mike, have they got you brainwashed yet?"

* In April 2016, Michael Conover was changed and convicted of attempting to possess and distribute Chinese-made MDMA—Ecstasy.

Mike glances up at the two of us and I can see he is not amused. He taps his temple with his pointer finger and says, "No, they finally got me thinking right." He abruptly picks us his tray and walks over to a table nearby full with RDAP members and takes a seat.

"Thanks Pete," I hiss, "now I'm gonna be standing up in that *fuckin'* meeting tomorrow." Pete's eyes jump between our two tables and he asks, what Mike's problem is. "Don't you get it? They got to 'im. The Michael Conover that you knew no longer exists. He is now a *Super*-Dapper."

The issue with being pulled-up, wasn't that I could potentially be removed from the program—I was within weeks of getting a management variable placed on me—it was, however, the interventions that always accompanied a pull-up.

Peers are required to delegate a way for you to "work on your struggle." These assignments are known as an "intervention." A peer may be forced to write a letter to their family explaining how they had jeopardized not only their sobriety, but also their year off over some salt. Or they would be required to write an apology letter to themselves and read it to their process group. Or any number of other ridiculous time-consuming, embarrassing assignments.

I was not pulled-up the next morning, but I did receive several uncomfortable glances from Conover.

Chapter Two

"I became insane with long intervals of horrible sanity."—Edgar Allen Poe

THE ATTITUDE CHECK AND THE RSA (Rational Self Analysis) are the foundation of the program. These two exercises are designed to help the participants recognize their thinking errors and instantaneously come up with a corrective solution to those negative thoughts. Basically, it's RDAP's way of reprogramming the "criminal thinking" of the participants; to get them to reason like a normal human being.

With that said, I have an issue with the structure of the RSA —it's overly complicated. Plus, I've never taken the workshops, therefore, I've never learned how to do an RSA. Instead, I write ten daily RSA's to fool the program's requirements. However, I do periodically write the required Attitude Checks.

So, for the readers' entertainment, I'm going to sprinkle a few of my Attitude Checks throughout the book.

"SO, ARE YOU A DRUGGIE?" asks my mom at our bi-monthly visit. We are sitting in the prison's visitation room surrounded by over fifty other felons. The room is large and loud. Half a dozen vending machines line one wall. There are bars on the windows.

My mother has noticed that I'm wearing a green rubber drug program bracelet around my wrist. As RDAP participants progress through each phase of the program they receive a colored band signifying their progress. Yellow is for inmates that have been placed in the RDAP housing unit, but have yet to start the program; green bands are assigned to first phase participants.

Then there's orange, white, and the elusive purple graduate band.

"But you don't even drink."

"I'm *only* taking it so the BOP doesn't move me, Mom." I'd been in the program for several months and we'd had this same discussion multiple times, but she's nearly ninety and skeptical of her con artist son. "It's more geared toward criminal thinking."

"Oh," she interjects, "you definitely have a problem with that." We share a smile and she continues, "you can be selfish (my mother does not hold back), just like your father."

ATTITUDE CHECK

MONDAY, JULY 17, 2017, I was called to visitation at 2:15 p.m., even though my mother had been waiting ever since 11:30 a.m. This irritated me. My mother is in a wheelchair and she is very uncomfortable. I can't believe how unprofessional and inefficient the BOP correctional officers are that work at visitation.

Which attitude was I struggling with- Humiliation.

After thinking about it, I realize that the correctional officers don't mean to be unprofessional retards. I shouldn't be irritated with them, they are just lazy and stupid. Only an idiot would work in a prison! I should feel bad for them.

Which attitude was I demonstrating- Open mindedness.

If I continue to utilize the program's tools to help me cope with my negative attitude, I will be a better person when I walk out of prison. If all goes well, I'll never have to see these morons again.

CONTENT GROUP is where RDAP participants discuss their daily assignments. It's crucial every inmate complete the seven journals (or workbooks). Today, however, Dr. Smith is sitting in on our group as we discuss our plans for re-entry.

For over thirty minutes I've been listening to my fellow peers discuss their lofty goals—rap stars, music producers, restaurateurs, et cetera. I'm just hoping the class ends before they get to me, but it doesn't.

"Mr. Cox," inquires The Doctor, "what're you're plans upon release?"

I don't want to sound grandiose. I want to be reasonable and humble, so I reply, "I expect that things will be difficult for me." I know it won't be easy, I have multiple felonies and I'm no longer able to work in the banking or real-estate industries. "I figure I'll have to bust my ass for at least a year, just to get my finances straight. Plus, I'm—"

"Wait a second," Dr. Smith interrupts, "you said one year; what happens if things don't improve within a year?"

"You mean if I'm still living in someone's spare room?" I reiterate, clarifying the question, but I already know my answer. "If I'm riding the bus to work and I can't pay my bills? If I'm on the verge of being homeless? I'm gonna commit a massive, massive fraud and leave the United States, because that's where I fucked up last time."

Brows shoot up among my peers and several submerge their faces into their hands. Others struggle not to laugh. Dr. Smith's mouth opens ever so slightly; however, she doesn't lead on that she's shocked by my answer.

"Crime should never be an option," she rebukes. "There's never—"

"Fraud is *always* an option," I interrupt. "Given the right circumstance *anyone* will commit a crime." That's not true, she tells me. Michelle Smith, PhD, with her smug upper-middleclass background, her two beautiful children, and her safe, secure government career, cannot conceive of an instance wherein she would commit a crime. "If the economy crashed and you ended up on the street—which *is* possible—and your family was living out of your car, your kids were bone-thin and there was a loaf of bread ten-feet inside a supermarket's front door, you'd steal that loaf of bread. You'd steal it to keep your kids alive for another day." As hard as she struggles, Dr. Smith can't maintain her smug look of pride and contempt. "The difference between *you* and *me*, Dr. Smith, is *my* threshold is lower."

She stares at me for a second too long and I understand she's irritated. She turns to the next member of the group and asks what his plans are for release.

"WHY'RE YOU GIVING THE DOCTOR a hard time?" asks Pete. We're walking the prison's half-mile-track. I can feel the shell crunching underneath my tennis shoes. The Florida sun is radiating down on us. The towers surrounding one of the complex's two penitentiaries are just on the other side of the barbed-wire fences. "Leave her alone," Pete continues, "just tell her what she wants to hear." I explain that I was being honest. It doesn't matter anyway, any day now the management variable will be placed on me. "What do you think of her, The Doctor?"

"Dr. Smith, she's something else," I reply. "She's kinda hot." Pete gives me a sideways glance. He thinks The Doctor is too thin. "She's a seven that jumps up to a nine the second she opens her mouth," I explain. "She's arrogant, but sexy as *fuckall*."

I'M SITTING IN CONTENT GROUP, when one of the orderlies tells me that the C-1 Unit counselor, Thompson, is looking for me. Thompson is a six foot four inches-tall shit-talking redneck with a massive gut. The last person I want to talk to.

I enter his office and he asks me to take a seat. Thompson informs me that my counselor, Counselor Thomas, is on vacation and he's handling Thomas' case load. "So," he says, "you've managed not to make one payment toward your FRP."

My chest immediately constricts and I instantly feel like I can't breathe. *Fuck!* I scream internally. I now realize he's holding a copy of my Judgement and Commitment and I knew, *I'm screwed.*

"FRP?" I ask, as if I'm not quite comprehending. "No has one's ever mentioned FRP..."

"Come on Cox, you know you owe six million in restitution." He admits that he's not quite sure how I've managed to stay off FRP refusal status, however, he informs me that that's all about to change.

Specifically, in order to be in the RDAP program, all participants must be current on their FRP payments. So, I'm in a really bad spot, and Thompson knows it.

Based on the amount of money I have deposited into my inmate account every month, he calculates that I can pay one hundred and eighty dollars in FRP per month.

"You can't be serious?!" I gasp. "I make twenty-five bucks

a month at my job and you want me to pay one hundred and eighty?"

"You get over three hundred dollars a month sent in," says Thompson. "Where's that coming from?"

The funds are a combination of money sent to me from my literary agent, friends, and my mother, but Thompson doesn't know that. "My mom sends me money," I admit. "So, are you telling me that you want my mom—who sends me money out of her social security stipend every month—to pay one hundred and eighty dollars a month toward *my* restitution?"

"Yes," he snaps. "Tell mom she's gotta pay one eighty or her little boy is going to get kicked outta the program and spend another year in prison and I'll make sure you don't get more than thirty days of halfway house."

I rear back and think, *What a dick!* "I'll do the extra year," I reply. "I'm not doing one eighty."

We stare at one another for a few seconds and Thompson agrees to work with me. We bounce a few figures around and eventually get to one hundred dollars per month.

"That's a gift Cox," he grunts. "Take it or leave it."

"I can do a hundred, but you've gotta give me some time. Can you start the payments in October?" I figure I should be out of the program by then and I'll just remove all of my funds before the debt hits.

"Alright Cox," he says, "I'll do October."

ATTITUDE CHECK

ON TUESDAY, AUGUST 1, 2017, the C-2 Counselor called me into his office and let me know that the BOP' central office has caught the fact that I owe $6 million. He then told me if I didn't start paying $100 a month he would put me on FRP refusal and I would be removed from RDAP. In addition, I would get 30 days halfway house. I'm extremely pissed off about it!

Which attitude was I struggling with- Willingness.

After thinking about the situation, I realized I did bilk multiple banks out of well over $55 million, and I do owe the $6 million.

Which attitude was I demonstrating- Responsibility.

If I continue working on my attitude, I will finish the program and—although I'll never pay off $6 million—I will make positive changes in my life. However, I'll most likely die of poverty. Go RDAP!

Chapter Three

"Many people hear voices when no one is there. Some of them are called mad and shut up in rooms where they stare at the walls all day. Others are called writers and they do pretty much the same thing."—Margaret Chittenden

PARTICIPATING IN THE PROGRAM is stressful. Physically stressful. Honestly, it's the only time during my incarceration I have even wanted to take a nap. It's not just me either. Program participants are sleeping in the library. Guys that have resisted using drugs their entire bid are sneaking into other housing units to smoke K2 or getting on antidepressants to cope with the stress.

Jackson confides in me that he regularly takes a one to two hour nap in the restroom's handicap stall.

ADMITTEDLY, I LEFT THE TAP ON as I brushed my teeth. I'm rhythmically stroking my molars when a senior peer says, "Hey, Mr. Cox, you gotta minute?"

I know the guy from my old housing unit. He's a crackhead that used to walk around the unit sucking on his fingers while rubbing his bellybutton—swear to God, it was one of the oddest things I've ever seen.

"Yeah, what's up?"

"The sink," he says, pointing to the faucet with his chin. "You can't be lettin' the sink run when you brush your teeth. You wastin' water." Ninety-eight percent of the water at the complex is recycled—we're actually drinking one another's urine. "You gotta shut it off . . . That'll get you pulled up."

"Seriously?" I didn't mean the request to shut off the

spigot. I understand he was either legitimately trying to help conserve the planet's resources—which is highly doubtful—or fishing for a pull-up. What I meant was, *Seriously, what kind of bizarro-world am I living in where this crackhead is telling me how to live my life.*

The following day the same junkie approaches me at the computer. He points to a sign above the station which reads: No Food or Beverages Near the Computers. He then points to my Diet Pepsi and says, "You can't be havin' no drinks around the computer, Mr. Cox."

"Seriously?"

ATTITUDE CHECK

FRIDAY, AUGUST 11, 2017, I was minding my own business when a peer—a crackhead—corrected me over something trivial. My first thought was, Who the fuck does this guy think he is?

Which attitude was I struggling with-Humility

After calming down, I realize that the peer has mental issues and I should be more patient with him. He can't help it that he's a pawn in the world of RDAP.

Which attitude was I demonstrating-Humility.

If I continue practicing these positive attitudes I will get through this program, and—although I don't see a need for the skill—I'll be able to deal with crackheads on the street.

GUYS ARE ALWAYS ASKING to read my stories. One particular guy, a black guy named William Davis, who looks remarkably like the actor Will Smith, has read everything I've written. On August 15, the night before I'm supposed to have my 60-day review (or "team") with Dr. Smith, all five DTS's, and—for moral support—several of my peers, Davis hands me back *Cash & Coke*, the last true crime he'd borrowed. It's the story of two brothers that were robbing drug dealers with the help of a dirty drug task force officer.

"I got a little pissed off at you when I read that." Davis tells me that he was offended by the fact that I'd described African-Americans as "savages" in the synopsis. I'm not exactly politically correct, however, I assure him I'm certain I wouldn't have done that. "I know what I read."

"Alright, well, I disagree," I reply. He's clearly agitated. I'm not inclined to defend myself against something I know I didn't write, so, we part ways.

The next day we're in content group discussing "loaded words" when DTS DeMille asks me if I ever use any. "Sure," I respond and she asks for an example. "Junkies. I say junkies all of the time."

Davis springs to his feet and bolts out of the class. Something's upset him. He is stopped outside by DTS Tabitha Anderson. She's a moderately attractive African-American woman who enjoys acting like she's "street," but I know she was raised middle-class. Regardless, she sees me as a privileged arrogant white male.

Anderson questions Davis as to why he's not in class. In his defense, Davis tries not to mention me specifically, but, eventually, he breaks and explains that he had an issue with what *he* described as my characterization of *all* black guys as savages.

The moment class was over, Davis told me that Anderson had flipped out and she was planning to bring up the issue during my team.

"What issue, bro?!" I snap. "That you're overly sensitive?" I retrieve the story and point out that I hadn't described the two robbers in the story as savages. In fact, they'd described themselves as savages and I'd simply repeated it in the narration. The offending text was a response to one of my main characters stating:

"I ain't some pussy ass cracka; I'm a real nigga. Know what I'm saying'?" In the narration I respond with: *I know what he's saying. I'd listened to him and his brother describe precisely what "real niggas" were. Specifically, they prided themselves on being brutal savages.*

That was it. That was what Davis had read that upset him. I quickly grab a copy of the story and point out *his* misunderstanding in regard to the meaning of my narration. He apologizes, but it's too late.

When I sit down in The Doctor's office with Davis and two other peers I instantly know it's not going to go well. Like a firing squad, Anderson, DeMille, Garcia, and two other DTS's are seated along one wall. Everyone but Garcia is glaring at me.

Davis immediately describes how he'd misunderstood what I'd written, however, Dr. Smith dismisses his explanation and Anderson expresses her concern that I might be a racist. She asks why I'm writing urban novels; I immediately explain that I don't write urban novels. "A novel by definition is fiction." In addition, urban novels are written in a guttural street vernacular. They are seldomly grammatically correct, and they're filled with sex and violence. "I write true crime stories, nonfiction."

"It's the same thing," she says dismissively—which is absolutely untrue. "Why write about crime?" she asks. I explain that I'm trying to reinvent myself as an author. I'd already had one book published and a second one was hitting Barnes & Nobles' shelves within a few months. But she waves the explanation off. "Urban novels glorify criminal behavior and I'm not sure that you should be writing them."

"First," I say, "I don't write urban novels, I write true crime, and second, you've never read any of my stories, so, you're not in a position to judge the content." I suggest that she peruse one of the synopses, but she declines.

Dr. Smith then pulls out my Pre-Sentence Report, a document which gives a brief overview of a prisoner's crimes as well as their addiction, family history, and the like. The report is typically 10 to 15 pages long, however, mine is over 100 pages and there's a 50-page supplemental document that chronicles my extensive fraud schemes. When I see it I know, *Things are about to go bad for me.*

"Who does this?" asks The Doctor, as she flips through the pages. Her face is dripping with disdain. All I can think about is getting out of the room. "Who are you Mr. Cox and why would you do all of this?"

I admit that I don't have a great answer for why I'd committed my crimes. DTS Anderson glances at me, runs her eyes up me—from my shoes to my eyes—and silently sneers. I can't believe it.

Christ, I think, *I've gotta get outta this room.*

"I've got some issues," I admit. Identifying issues, the damaging consequences of those issues, and how the inmates are working on modifying their behavior in regard to their issues is a constant theme of the program.

"And what are your issues, Mr. Cox?" she asks. Caring, I tell her. "Caring," she queries, "caring about what?"

"Your opinion of me, for one thing." Look, I was almost outta the program and it just slipped out.

Not only does The Doctor look stunned, but so do my peers as well as the DTS's. In fact, Anderson shoots me a nasty look and gives me the onceover, *again.* This time, however, I look her up and down and scoff. Her eyes bulge slightly in disbelief.

Davis tries to come to my aid, stating how well I'm doing in our group, but Dr. Smith waves him off. "Tell me about your father," she asks; at the mention of my father the walls began to close in on me. "He was an alcoholic, wasn't he?"

"He was a drunk," I concede. Arrogant, self-centered, and verbally abusive; he used to get liquored-up and call my sisters bitches and whores. My brother and I were worthless and stupid. To this day I can still hear the gravel in his voice as he told me, *You'll never amount to anything.* "My father was unconcerned with how his actions affected others," I inform her. "It's all in my PSI."

"You're a lot like him, aren't you?" She's trying to unsettle me. It's becoming hard to breathe in the room and I'm desperate to escape. I don't want to discuss my father and our relationship. The time he showed up to my soccer game drunk and humiliated me. The vicious comments and disappointment. "I can be a selfish prick at times," I respond flippantly. "There's no denying it."

She doesn't get the reaction she wants. In retaliation, Dr. Smith assigns me an intervention wherein I have to write a two page essay defining the term "selfish prick." The meeting is over.

As I walk out of the door, The Doctor stops me. "Mr. Cox, the urban novels..." she says with a smug grim, "they're a waste of time."

Dr. Smith wants me to forget my dream and get a job at Walmart. Dr. Smith wants me to humble myself and live a lower-middleclass existence. Dr. Smith wants me to die in obscurity.

ATTITUDE CHECK

MONDAY, AUGUST 22, 2017, I was frustrated with my cellie, Ledford. The guy is always bugging me about ironing my clothes and doing my homework. I just want to be left alone!

Which attitude was I struggling with-Humility.

Once I'd thought about what my Super-Dapper, Kool-Aid drinking, cult member cellie said, I realized that I am in RDAP and I need to keep my clothes looking sharp. He just wants me to pass the program, and, deep, deep, deep down, I know he's right.

Which attitude was I demonstrating-Open mindedness.

If I continue to think positively I will complete the program and maybe I'll make some positive changes in my flawed thinking.

Chapter Four

"They call it Stockholm syndrome ... I had no free will until I was separated from them for about two weeks."—Patty Hearst

IT'S AUGUST 24, 2017, during the morning meeting, and I'm wedged deep into the sea of my RDAP peers. Dr. Smith is mildly annoyed. The unit orderlies—her obedient informants, her minions, her henchmen—have brought it to her attention that the program participants *sometimes* leave their cups in the TV room or their soap dishes next to the sinks. It's not a big deal, but she's making it into one.

The Doctor has several items—cups, bowls, some plastic wear, a t-shirt, and a clear plastic shower bag with an assortment of hygiene products in it—resting on a table in the center of the room. She asks if anyone recognizes the items as theirs, they should come get them. Everyone knows it's a trap and if they admit to having left the items they will most likely get extra duty for "cognitive indolence"—lazy thinking.

She slips on a pair of clear plastic gloves and holds up the shower bag. She prances around the rooms with the bags held over her head like a high ring model displaying a round card to a crowd of boxing fans. "Does anyone recognize this," she asks. No one recognizes it, of course. She pulls out several of the items: a bar of soap, a razor, and a photograph wrapped in tape —waterproofed for use in the shower. The picture depicted a girl staring longingly into the camera. Her legs are spread and she's wearing nothing but socks. "Are you guys telling me that no one recognizes this young lady." Dr. Smith flashes the photo to the group. *What's with the socks?* I ask myself. "Clearly," The Doctor continues, "whoever's picture this is, you've obviously had a relationship with her for a *very* long time."

No one moves to claim the bag. At this point it would be suicide. Dr. Smith is now furious that someone in the room is lying.

Then, a big black guy—one of Dr. Smith's orderlies—stands up and addresses the community. "Come on man," he says. "The day after I found that in the showers one of you guys came to me and asked if I'd found it." Unfortunately, he'd already turned the bag in to The Doctor. "Show some integrity, don't make me point you out."

Suddenly, Brandon Elkins * shoots up from his seat and yelps, "I'd like to take responsibility for the shower bag!"

* On September 23, 2016, Brandon Elkins was sentenced to 72 months for receipt of child pornography.

Multiple inmates manage to suppress their amusement, nonetheless I burst into laughter. *What an idiot.* The peers beside me shush me, but I ignore them.

Dr. Smith gives Elkins four weeks of restroom duty—scrubbing down the showers and toilets—and I'm pretty certain he was forced to repeat part of the program. This is known as being "rephased."

IT'S NOT UNCOMMON FOR PARTICIPANTS to slip notes informing on one another underneath Dr. Smith's or one of the DTS's office doors. At some point, given the right set of circumstances, prisoners will begin to sympathize and even care for their captors. The hostage will even begin to side with their abductors. In many instances, they will help their captors for no other reason than the benefit of their jailers. This is known as Stockholm syndrome.

Pete and I are discussing the abnormality over dinner, when he says, "It's done to curry favor. It's self-preservation."

"No," I reply, "because most of the time the prisoners will continue to argue in favor of their abductors weeks and months after they've been released." The victims will be perfectly safe in their own homes with the hostage takers in custody and yet the victims will continue to side with them. "Pete, I'm watching it right now; some of these guys aren't even getting the year off… There's no benefit to them."

"What's your problem with the program?"

"I just don't understand why it's designed to turn the R-Dappers against each other," I reply. There are plenty of successful drug treatment programs that don't require the patients to co-operate against one another. "That's all I'm saying."

In general, being in the program causes a constant psychological stress. There's a cult atmosphere to it. Every action is controlled by the staff, senior peers or comps. There is always someone watching.

"I understand," says Pete. "They have complete control over you; like when the Symbionese Liberation Army kidnapped Patty Hearst (in early-1974)."

"Right, right, exactly." After being kept in a closet for several weeks and forced to read Symbionese Liberation Army propaganda around the clock, Hearst became convinced of her captors' cause. She even went so far as to rob a bank with them. When she was eventually arrested (or rescued) she had been so thoroughly brainwashed that she called out support for her "brothers and sisters in the revolution." In fact, she listed her occupation as "urban guerrilla fighter."

Pete laughs at this and says, "I didn't know about the urban guerrilla thing."

"It's not that hard to brainwash someone," I continue. "These guys have Stockholm syndrome."

"MR. COX, PLEASE COME TO MRS. DEMILLE'S office," bellows the overhead speakers throughout the unit. I'm pretty sure I know what this is about.

My group is transitioning from the Orientation journal to the Rational Thinking journal, and each of our books have to be perused by our class DTS. Because this wasn't something I'd anticipated, I'd answered the bulk of the questions within the books honestly. For example, when asked: What makes it difficult for you to maintain an attitude of open-mindedness? I stated: *I'm in a hostile environment with prisoners that don't care about me and are actively trying to jam me up—i.e. pull-ups. It's not a lack of open-mindedness, it's acute environmental-awareness and self-preservation.* When asked: What will your life look like in 10 years if you stop your drug use behavior. What impact will it have on your... family? I answered: *Let's see, I'll be 58 in ten years, I like to think I'll be dating a hot 28-year-old blonde ex-stripper gold-digger with no kids that's only interested in me for my vast real estate fortune. No family, just me and the gold-digger. That's the prefect chick for me.* ...work? I answered: *I'm planning on opening a chain of rooming houses for sex offenders, which I'll call "eco-units." I'll make a fucking fortune.* ...role in the community? I answered: *Are you serious? Once the eco-units take off I'll be even more despised than I am now. But money is the great equalizer, so I'll be fine.* ...finances? I answered: *Sweet!* ...health? I answered: *Assuming the hot blonde bombshell ex-stripper gold-digger girlfriend doesn't kill me in bed, I should be in pretty good shape.*

So, when I enter DeMille's office to pick up my journal, I expect to be read the riot act; instead she hands me my book and says, "Keep up the good work Mr. Cox, you're doing a great job."

There wasn't one page that wasn't covered with outrageous answers. *Huh*, I think, *she didn't even look at it.*

ATTITUDE CHECK

WEDNESDAY, SEPTEMBER 1, 2017, my Big Brother (the guy that is supposed to be shepherding me through the program) realized that I've been turning in my Attitude Checks without him ever seeing or approving them. He got even more upset when he realized I'd been signing his name. What is your problem? I tell him. It's not my fault you're never around. He got even more upset when he saw what I'd been writing. Talk about ungrateful!

Which attitude was I struggling with- Open mindedness.

After thinking about it, I could have gotten him in trouble because he's supposed to be helping me. Plus, it's my responsibility to find him. It's not his fault that I'd been signing his name.

Which attitude was I demonstrating- Open mindedness and Responsibility.

If I continue to practice these positive attitudes I will exit prison a responsible person. Go RDAP!

THE HUMILIATION DYNAMIC is used almost exclusively during the morning meeting. Other than the pull-ups, as a part of the program all of the inmates must participate in the morning meeting. Like a performing monkey, at some point they must read short summaries of news articles or act as a facilitator; randomly choosing participants to speak about "the word of the day" or give "positive praise" to the other prisoner. Regardless, at one point or another as a participant you will be standing in front of one hundred and fifty peers performing.

My favorite humiliation, is the "up-beat ritual," wherein the program participants must partake in a group game of some sort. Guys are chosen to do any number of humiliating things; the games range from revealing something embarrassing about themselves to recite the philosophy using the voice of Daffy Duck or Kermit the Frog. The punishments for failure or not performing well, might be anything from having to do the chicken-dance to singing "happy birthday to me" while patting themselves on the head and spinning like a ballerina.

We are told by Dr. Smith that the purpose of the upbeat ritual is to get us to lower our guards and to "get out of your boxes." However, I believe it's just one of the many ways the program is designed to breakdown the psyche.

During one of our many discussions regarding the program, Pete mentions that all militaries break new recruits' psyches down in order to rebuild them. "First, they isolate the recruits; they tell them when to sleep, eat, use the bathroom, everything. Then the drill sergeants systematically breakdown the recruits' identities to the point where it doesn't work in their current environment. Then they replace it with another set of behaviors, attitudes, and beliefs that work in the environment. It's not that hard, plus most of the RDAP guys have an incentive."

"Yeah, but in the military, they build you into a lethal weapon." I laugh, "In RDAP they're turning these guys into lambs."

"That's not true," snaps Pete. He's right, of course. Moreover, most of the guys need the program and make huge strides dealing with their addictions, antisocial issues, and personal demons. However, in my current situation it's hard to admit.

Chapter Five

"Before you diagnose yourself with depression or low self-esteem, first make sure that you are not, in fact, just surrounding yourself with assholes."—William Gibson

I'M STARTING TO GET NERVOUS. It's September 8, 2017, my treatment plan is due in four days and I haven't done one assignment. Luckily, that same day, my case manager informs me that the Bureau has placed the management variable on me. I'm no longer at risk of being transferred to a camp. Immediately, I scribble out a note to Dr. Smith stating that I want to sign out of the program and I slip it underneath her office door.

Unlike most of the guys requesting to be removed from the program. The Doctor does not call me in to her office. In fact, she never even acknowledges my request. It takes three weeks before I'm finally removed from the program and sent back to my old housing unit.

When I enter the unit, the first thing I see is a tiny little transgender-female that, I swear to God, looks exactly like a fourteen-year-old girl. "Erica" can't be but five foot tall with pigtails. The transgender is perched on a locker, kicking "her" feet while singing along at full volume to Taylor Swift's *We are Never Getting Back Together.*

The transgender is so convincingly female in appearance, my first thought is, *How the fuck did that little girl get in here.*

LET ME TELL YOU ABOUT THE B-4 CASE MANAGER. Her name is Jennifer Agard. * She is an amazingly polite and friendly person, albeit lazy and ineffective. She is the quintessential bureaucrat.

_{* First name has been changed.}

When I enter her office on September 22, 2017, the day I'd been transferred back to the unit, she is leaning back in her chair sipping from a mug of coffee. "Can I help you, Cox?"

"Yes, ma'am," I reply. I explain that I wasn't sure which bed I'd been assigned. I had been given a "bed book card" and a printout regarding my transfer. However, one states I've been assigned a two man cell and the other states I'm assigned to a large surplus-room known as "the fish bowl." This room holds five bunkbeds and smells like feet. "The issue is it looks like both beds are occupied in the two man cell." She stares at me with a blank indifference on her face, so, I clarify the problem, "Sometimes guys will make up the beds so they look like they're occupied, when they're actually empty . . . You know, so they can have the cell to themselves, and, well, I'd rather not have to sleep in the fishbowl."

"Okay," says Agard, "sooo . . . what do you want me to do; walk down there and check for you? I mean, I'm sitting here, relaxing." She raises her mug slightly. "I have my coffee. I'm winding down my day—I leave in an hour . . ." Once again, she stares at me with indifference.

"I guess I could just go to the fishbowl—"

"Let's do that!" she snaps.

I have to laugh at the blatant laziness of Case Manager Agard and she knowingly smiles back at me. *Fucking BOP staff*, I tell myself, *you've gotta love 'em.*

IN EARLY-OCTOBER, MY FRP PAYMENT comes due. I've drained my account so that when the BOP attempts to debit the payment it bounces. Sometime around noon the computer automatically places me on FRP refusal status, but it doesn't matter. My locker is full of coffee, creamers, and granola bars—that's all I need to survive—and I'm already sleeping in the fishbowl, so I can't be moved to a less desirable sleeping area. It doesn't get less desirable than the fishbowl.

Life is good.

EVERYTHING IS WORKING OUT. I'm able to complete *Devil Exposed*, the twisted tale of an LA kingpin who was framed for the murder of two FBI informants. I then turn my attention to a story I'd been struggling with surrounding a baby-faced nineteen-year-old college student who ended up trafficking cocaine for multiple cartels.

Plus, I'm able to finish up the quarter's Real Estate ACE (Adult Continuing Education) course. The inmates' case managers require them to participate in at least one ACE course per quarter. I've been teaching the course for over a decade. It's a basic course on real estate, however, the prison doesn't actually pay me. So, to compensate for this, I sell the completion-certificates to those guys that don't actually want to take the class. Because the inmates aren't allowed to have cash, I typically get two coffees and two creamers, which is the equivalent of ten dollars.

Most of the time I get paid. However, in December 2017, one of my students kept stalling on payment. He's a six-foot two-inch behemoth black guy that everyone, appropriately calls "Big Dummy."

Physically, he's massive, however, he is the mental equivalent of an eight-year-old. Powerful, but harmless. The last day of class I refuse to give him his certificate. "You never paid me, bro," I explain.

"Cox," he retorts, with this big fake smile, "I got your stuff in the unit. I'll give it to you later. But I need the certificate now, 'cause . . . you know, I got like team and shit tomorrow."

I tell him that's not a problem, we can go to the unit and grab the stuff right now. Ten minutes later, I enter his cell. As I hand him the certificate he hands me a two dollar bag of potato chips.

"This isn't what I asked for," I say. "Where's the coffee and creamers—"

"Fuck you!" snaps Big Dummy and he chuckles at having gotten over on me. "You fuckin' con man."

I immediately act like I'm going to sling the bag of chips down the hallway. Being the fat blob-of-shit that he is, Big Dummy's eyes instinctively follow the bag trajectory. The moment he looks away, I snatch the certificate out of his hand, turn and walk away.

I'm sitting in my chair a few minutes later when this buffoon stomps into my cell. He frantically glances around the room and grunts, "I need that certificate."

I pull the certificate from underneath my pillow and tell him to bring me two coffees and two creamers and I will gladly give him the certificate. Unfortunately, he reaches for it, which causes me to immediately tear up the certificate. This causes Big Dummy to screech like a girl, "What'd you do!"

"Listen stupid," I say. "Calm down and go get me two fucking bags of coffee and two creamers, and I'll make you another certificate tomorrow morning."

He finally realizes he doesn't have a choice and gets the commissary items. This is the type of stupidity I deal with on a daily basis.

"I NEED TO TALK TO YOU," says Cesar Kou Reyna, a Peruvian national doing time for conspiracy to commit bank fraud. During my time in RDAP he and I became close friends. Unfortunately for Cesar, he is still stuck in the program and enraged at the fact that his big brother, a particularly creepy sex offender, David Laist, * intentionally sabotaged Cesar during his team. Specifically, Laist told Dr. Smith that, in his opinion, Cesar wasn't ready to move on to the third phase of the program. Remarkably, based on Laist's opinion, The Doctor re-phased Cesar. "I want him outta the program. Every day I see him I wanna smash his face."

---

* In 2014 David Laist was indicted for possession of child pornography. The following year he was sentenced to 72 months.

Cesar is angry and, like most people are prone to do, he is quenching his irritation by plotting his revenge. He goes over multiple scenarios that could *potentially* get Laist removed from the unit. However, none seem all that promising.

"Look," I reply, "Laist is Dr. Smith's golden boy; she's not kicking him out on a whim. It's gotta be substantive." I agree to think about the issue. "But It's doubtful you're getting him thrown out."

Maybe a week later, a few days into the new year, I see Laist walking the compound with an inmate named Richard Lee—another sex offender as well as one of Dr. Smith's favorite comps.* Lee is a South Korean that fancies himself an aristocrat, and, for reasons unknown to me, he dislikes Cesar who is half-Peruvian, half-Chinese. Consequently, I sense an opportunity.

* In 2015 Richard Lee was indicted for possession of child pornography; later that same year he was sentenced to 48 months.

"Have you guys seen Cesar?" I ask.

I'm fully prepared to make a crack at Cesar's expense, in the hopes of coaxing Laist and Lee into reciprocating, however, Lee immediately begins making derogatory comments and then, Laist jumps in.

"Why do you hang out with him?" asks Lee. "The guy's a fucking peasant." It's a comment unique to Lee and I make a mental note to incorporate it.

Laist, jumps into the Cesar-bashing feet first. "Yeah," he says with a chuckle, "is he paying you to hang-out with him or something?"

"Yeah," adds Lee, "Laist almost got him kicked outta the program."

They both laugh, as if the statement is hilarious. Why they're so openly willing to bash a guy that I am *clearly* friends with, can most aptly be explained using the RDAP term, super-optimism. They simply believe they are untouchable. Bulletproof. I can't help but think, *What a couple of clowns these two are.* I visualize myself slapping them both across their faces. This makes me grin.

I'm sitting in the library later that night when I see Davis. I call him over and casually mention the exchange between myself, Laist, and Lee. Davis immediately asks if I would mind him mentioning it to Dr. Smith.

"Kind of..." I reply. I tell Davis that Dr. Smith is extremely fond of both Laist and Lee, therefore, "the smart move is to just pull them up for lack of caring, manipulation, and breaking confidentiality. That'll force Dr. Smith's hand; she'll have to do something about them."

At this point Davis begins nodding his agreement and he asks, "And you'll back me up if she calls you in?"

"Of course."

Cesar tracks me down at the cafeteria, roughly a week later. He is giddy with excitement. As it turns out, Davis had pulled-up both Laist and Lee and they vehemently denied that they had spoken to me about Cesar. However, Dr. Smith didn't believe them.

"I can't believe you pulled that off," says Cesar.

Within a day or two, Lee was moved to his old housing unit. Laist, however, was stripped of his comp responsibilities and required to begin attending process groups.

When Cesar informs me that Laist had been allowed to remain in the RDAP Unit, I'm a little disappointed. I immediately tell him I'm ready to finish the job, but Cesar insists that Laist has been neutralized. "There's no reason to do anything else."

APPROXIMATELY, THE SAME TIME, Ashworth—the tatted-up methamphetamine trafficker—tells me that the little terrorist, Jackson, has been high on Suboxone going on a month straight. He's been on and off of the stuff since entering the program, however, the prolonged presence of the drug in his system is causing him to become paranoid. He's so suspicious, Jackson has got it into his head that others in the program are plotting against him... more so than normal.

Specifically, Ashworth tells me that Jackson is focusing his suspicion on him. Despite numerous people telling him that Ashworth isn't plotting against him Jackson can't be reasoned with.

"That little junky's paranoid like a motherfucker," says Ashworth, while we're standing outside commissary. "He's gonna end up getting himself thrown out of the program."

Then, a couple weeks before Ashworth's group—my old group—graduates, Jackson overhears Ashworth talking to another peer. Due to Ashworth having issues in the past with holding his peer accountable, he says, he feels like he needs to do one more pull-up to prove to Dr. Smith that he deserved to graduate.

Jackson, in his paranoid state of delirium, tells Mike Rodger * that Ashworth is trying to fake his way through the program and suggested that Mike pull him up for manipulation.

* Last name has been changed.

The next morning, shortly before graduation, Mike stands up in the morning meeting and announces, "I'd like to address Mr. Ashworth."

The whole time Mike is laying out the accusation in front of the community and several peers give feedback, Jackson is sitting in the crowd nodding his head emphatically and smiling. This sends Ashworth into a rage and when it's time for him recite the pull-up's content and interventions, he stumbles.

One of the DTS's tells Ashworth, "Take your time and focus."

"How am I supposed to *focus* with this little fucker smiling at me like that?!" yells Ashworth; and with the outburst, Ashworth lost any chance of graduating.

Dr. Smith re-phased him the following day.

IN EARLY-FEBRUARY 2018 my case manager, Agard, inopportunely tells me that the Bureau has removed my management variable.

"You said it was good for a year," I gasp.

"Usually that's true, but there's a big push to move inmates to camps," she shrugs, "and you have camp points, so—"

I struggle for a solution, unfortunately, I know there's only one way to stop the move. "You can't ship me, I'm going back to RDAP." Agard asks when this had happened and I reply, "Dr. Smith's moving me sometime next week."

"Okay, well... I'll hold the paperwork."

I immediately send The Doctor a request to be placed in the next class and she schedules me for a "clinical team" the following week.

On the second to the last Wednesday of the month I find myself seated in front of Dr. Smith while flanked by the program DST's, including: Andrew, DeMille, and Garcia.

"I'm not sure why I should consider allowing you back into the program, Mr. Cox," says The Doctor. It had never once occurred to me that Dr. Smith wouldn't accept me. She reminds me that the last time I was in the program I'd shown little interest in changing. "Can you give me one reason why I should let you back into RDAP?"

DTS Anderson sneers at me—it only lasts for a millisecond, but I catch it—and I know I've got a problem. So, I reach down into the vault for something they'll believe, something genuine, something the average inmate wouldn't admit. Something disturbing.

I lean forward and clear my throat. "Honestly, I'm not sure I have a drug problem (I'm actually one hundred percent certain I don't), but I know I've got a serious cognitive issue." I tell her that the closer I get to my release date the more anxious I feel. You see, I'm no longer allowed to work in any of the industries that I have experience in, finance, real estate or development. According to my probation restrictions, they're all off-limits. I look her in the eye and say, "When I can't sleep at night, you know what calms my anxiety ... *fraud*. When I lay in my bunk and wonder what's going to become of me and it gets to be too much, I start planning a scam. Everything from how I'll get the identities to which bank I'll hit first."

When I inform The Doctor and the DTS's that the mere thought of it is so comforting to me that I fall asleep before I ever take a dollar out of the bank, Dr. Smith's brow raises a fraction of inches and I know I've got her.

"Now, I'm pretty sure that's not normal," I concede. "So, if I have to come down here and take some crap from you guys for nine months to try and fix it, then that's what has to happen."

Dr. Smith shifts her weight forward and begins pecking away at her keyboard. "I'm going to get you in the next class Mr. Cox," she says and I almost laugh.

That's how I end up *back* in RDAP on March 22, 2018—the same date my original group graduates the program.

ATTITUDE CHECK

FRIDAY, MARCH 23, 2018, I got irritated when a peer stood outside my cell and yelled to one of his friends down the hallway. What happened to not screaming in the fucking unit? This place has gone to shit since the last time!!!

Which attitude was I struggling with- Humility

After thinking about it, I realized that his behavior will haunt him the rest of his life. It's unlikely that he will truly excel in any legal industry. He will most likely get out and sell drugs again and end up back in prison. That gives me a certain satisfaction.

Which attitude was I demonstrating- Open mindedness.

If I continue to practice these positive attitudes I will be able to maintain my sanity in the face of unadulterated stupidity and, eventually, I'll make it out of prison. Once outside, I will be separated from idiots like the screamer.

Chapter Six

"I am a spy in the house of me. I report back from the front lines of the battle that is me. I am somewhat bewildered by the event that is my life."—Carrie Fisher

"I'M A LITTLE CONCERNED ABOUT THE LETTER," I admit to Pete at dinner. One of the invasive exercises conducted by the DTS's running the program is the request of participants' families to mail in a letter stating how your drug behavior and crimes negatively affected them. "My mom is almost ninety. I can't send it to her. My sisters and brother will absolutely *not* lie for me (by stating I have a drug problem)."

"You dodged the letter last time," replies Pete, as he pulls a small plastic pill bottle of seasoning out of his pocket. He offers me some of the seasoning, but I shake my head in the negative. We are surrounded by half of the participants in the program.

"Look around Pete," I say. "These guys are everywhere."

He chuckles and says, "You can't have seasoning?"

Coleman doesn't allow inmates to bring anything into or out of the cafeteria—that includes seasoning. Despite the fact that the food is extremely bland and they hardly ever have salt or pepper. As a result, the prisoners will actually sneak in seasoning they've purchased at commissary.

"If I take a fucking grain of that, five guys are gonna pull me up tomorrow morning. I shit you not."

Pete finds my dilemma extremely entertaining. Nearly every day I have a different drama to report on. None have anything to do with me. Still, I am concerned about the letter. I knew during my last stint that I wasn't going to be in the program for the final phase, and therefore I wouldn't be required to mail a letter to anyone. This time, however, I may have to go a few weeks into the third phase. Ergo, the letter is an issue.

Pete suggests I tell the staff that I have no family, but they have my Pre-Sentence Investigation Report, email and phone records as well as my visitation log. "They'll know it's bullshit."

"Your ex-wife," announces Pete. "Call Keyla and explain the situation; have them send her the letter." It's not a bad idea. My ex-wife is remarried and has three children from her new husband, however, she still comes to see me and we talk on the phone often.

That night, I'm standing at the bank of phones when Keyla answers. Immediately, doing my best imitation of a black guy, I snap, "What up *baby-momma?!*"

She laughs, "What up *baby-daddy?*" I quickly explain the situation regarding the letter and ask her if I can have the staff mail the instructions to her. "So, you need me to write a letter explaining how your criminal behavior negatively affected me in the past?"

"Well, yeah, but . . ." something feels really wrong about the way she phrased the statement and I say, "Look, don't get crazy oaky? It doesn't have to—"

"Send the letter!" she snaps. "I've been waiting fifteen years to write that fucking letter."

"Oh Christ! Come on Keyla, don't do this to me."

MY NEW GROUP is made up of pure madness. There is Calvis Robinson, a bone thin black guy with dreads. Due to his religion—some form of Voodoo—he refuses to bathe. *Disgusting!* The group's got two con men—three if you include me—Joseph Vitale and (eventually) Thomas Guerriero. All of us are incarcerated for various fraud related charges. We all suffer from "grandiosity" and varying degrees of narcissism. Then there's Todd Dorsett, a Florida farmer caught growing over ten tons of marijuana. Plus, the normal ensemble of thuggish drug dealers—Ivanhoe Butler, Peterson Fils-Aime, Tyron Jackson, and so on—and one huge flamboyant gay oxy dealer named Cleon Major. Then, there's the transgender-female, Gregory Martin,* or (as we are instructed to refer to inmate Martin) "Miss Martin."

* Name has been changed.

DTS Anderson is our content DTS, and she looks amused when she notices me sitting in her class, surrounded by twenty other inmates. "It looks like we're going to be spending the next three months together," she says to the class. Then, Anderson grins at me and ads, "What do you think about that Mr. Cox; ninety days of me?"

"Cool," is all I manage to get out. *This woman thinks I'm a racist*, I tell myself. *She despises me.*

I keep my head down and try to make myself invisible, but it's no use. Anderson calls on me every chance she gets. I am absolutely miserable and she is reveling in my despondency.

At the end of the content group, as my fellow peers and I shuffle out of the classroom, DTS Anderson asks, "So, Mr. Cox, what'd you think of the group?"

I glance up, smirk, and say, "One down, eighty-nine more days to go."

She squeezes her eyelids into a glare, but says nothing.

DAYS AFTER I START RDAP, I'm talking with Cesar. We're waiting in the cafeteria line along with around two hundred other inmates. Cesar and I are deep in a discussion regarding whether I am required to call the transgender "Miss Martin."

"Dr. Smith said you've gotta call her Miss Martin," says Cesar, "and you have to use the female pronoun—"

"Get the fuck outta here! She can't make me call this guy *her*."

"She can do whatever she wants."

A prisoner, William Duff, a massive, six-foot plus, black guy, who'd just graduated the program is standing directly behind us as well as several other peers. Duff makes a smart ass crack to Cesar, but Cesar ignores him. Oddly, Duff becomes disproportionately offended and calls Cesar a punk.

I turn to Duff and ask, "What are you getting so pissed off about, bro?"

Duff pokes his finger in my direction and barks, "Turn your *bitch ass* around before I beat your fuckin' punk ass!" At this, several people turn around and gawked at the scene. I can't believe that he just called me a bitch. Rage rushes over me—you don't call another man a bitch in prison—however, Duff is an enormous guy with a *major* anger management problem and I'm five-foot seven-inches tall with a good pair of shoes. I'm no idiot, so, I fight my anger and slowly turn around.

This infuriates Duff and he storms out of the cafeteria.

Cesar and I talked about the incident over lunch. I was furious and Cesar suggested I "confront and level" with Duff once I calmed down. "Work the program," he says. Because I'd never paid attention during my last stint in RDAP, Cesar has to walk me through the steps of a confront and level. "If he's not receptive to the confrontation . . . you can pull him up."

That night Cesar, myself, and two senior peers approach Duff regarding the incident in the cafeteria. He downplays the whole incident and twists the facts; however, he does give Cesar and I a half-assed acceptance of responsibility. Regardless, I won't let it go and he can see that.

The next morning during the morning meeting, when the facilitator asks "are there any pull-ups," I raise my hand, but he doesn't call on me. Duff sees this and, later that day, I find out that he's trying to convince another comp to pull me up and state that he'd overheard me and Cesar discussing plans to commit fraud upon our release; which was total bullshit. Unfortunately for Duff, the comp he spoke to was Davis—the Will Smith look-alike. Although, Davis refused to play along, I realize that doesn't mean that Duff won't convince another comp. So, the following morning I raise my hand again, but the facilitator passes me over, as well as the next day.

On April 2, 2018, the facilitator asks if I'd like to address someone? "Yeah," I reply. Bear in mind, I'm encircled by one hundred and fifty inmates making me uncharacteristically nervous. "I'd like to address Mr. Duff."

Duff feigns a confused look as he stands. Knowing he'd been trying to sabotage me for the past few days, my anxiety immediately turns to rage and I declare, "Last Tuesday, we were standing in the chow hall line—*two days* after you graduated the program—and you verbally attacked me." As I recount the incident I become more and more animated. Several peers call out "stick with the format," but I don't know the format and I angrily wave them off. From the corner of the room I can see one of the DTS's grin at this. I continue to rail against Duff and I can see fear seeping into his eyes. Understand, even after an inmate has passed the program, Dr. Smith has the authority to fail an inmate—even after they've graduated—thereby adding the one year reduction for graduating back onto their sentence. "Here's the thing, Duff," I snap, "I can't even give you an intervention; I'm so pissed off, it wouldn't be coming from a place of caring." I catch my breath and end with, "The one silver lining is this, I'm now one hundred percent certain that I can fake my way through the program... cause you just did."

A murmur ripples through the community. Duff looks like his legs are going to buckle as he realizes that I may have very well cost him his year (I didn't, by the way). However, within a week, he and I are sitting in our process group when I address him again. This time my attack on him is so venomous, the following morning, Duff asks to be transferred out of the unit. Davis later tells me that Duff confided he was worried he wouldn't survive another confrontation with me.

"SO, WHO WOULD YOU *FUCK*?" asks Casey Padula. Incarcerated for tax evasion, Padula is the newest member of RDAP, as well as the Narcissists' Circle, comprised of Guerriero, Vitale, and myself.

He wants to know, given the opportunity, which of the female DTS's each of us would have sex with. Guerriero immediately zeros in on Wilkerson, an attractive churchy African-American with the kind of curves you don't see on an Anglo. Vitale is in full agreement. Padula, to everyone's shock, chooses Anderson.

"Are you serious?" interjects Vitale. "She's such a bitch."

"I know," agrees Padula. "I'd love to grudge-fuck that condescending look off her face."

The group shares a laugh and Guerriero announces, "Cox has a thing for The Doctor. You'd do Doc, right?" I tell him that, if I had to choose, it would unquestionably be Dr. Smith. She has a whole Zoe Saldana thing going on, however, I'm not interested in her. "I thought you liked the skinny ones?"

"Yeah, well I grew up in central Florida; it's the trailer park capital of the world, so, yeah, I'm partial to dirty-foots, but Doc, nah." I explain that Dr. Smith is simply too smart to date. She's too manipulative. "I feel for her ex-husband, poor guy probably never won an argument, *ever*. I like a smart chick, but not one that's smarter than me."

Chapter Seven

"If you are always trying to be normal, you will never know how amazing you can be."—Maya Angelou

JUST AFTER 10:00 A.M., on April 12, 2018, the new cell rotation is placed on the wall in the front of the unit. Fortunately, I wasn't moved, however, when I get back to my cell, Miss Martin, the six-foot tall transgender-female with long thin braids—baring a striking resemblance to Serena Williams—is standing between the single bed and the bunkbed.

"Ohmigod Cox, isn't this great," she shrieks, "we're gonna be cellies!"

"Well, well," I stammer in an all-consuming disbelief, "I'm not happy about it." I stomp off to meet Cesar in the cafeteria; leaving Miss Martin standing in the cell with a look of dejection.

By the time we sit down with our plates of fried chicken —the only decent meal of the week—I'm burning up with rage. Cesar, the ceaseless peacemaker, is desperately trying to calm me down. I'm certain that Dr. Smith has placed the tranny in my room as a sick joke. "Okay," shouts Cesar over the other inmates' chatter, "so, what are you gonna do?"

"I'm, I'm—"

"You're not going to drop outta the program, so don't even say it." He then mentions the fact that I'd be shipped immediately, and that would kill my mother. "Plus, you're working on two stories right now." I'd just finished *The Unlikely Narco*; the story of Jacob Diaz, the baby-faced American college student that had ended up an operative for the Mexican cartels. In addition, I was a week into Joseph Vitale's story. Vitale was one of the members of the Narcissists Circle. As a former high pressure broker in South Florida, Vitale had somehow gotten himself entangled in multiple scams, two murders, and a federal indictment.

"Fuck!" I spat. My main concern was that, if I remained in the cell with Miss Martin, I'd have to take crap from my fellow inmates. "I can't do it."

"Yes, you can," sighs Cesar. "Look, don't let Dr. Smith run you out of the program." Cesar tells me I have two choices, "one, you act like a jerk and complain about Miss Martin—which isn't going to change anything—or, two, you accept it." That's more my style and he knows it. "Get your head straight and embrace the challenge."

"God damnit," I groan. He is absolutely right.

Just before four o'clock count, I walk into my cell and see Miss Martin sitting on her bunk. She looks a little sad, until I shoot her a big smile, and gasp, "Kitten! I want to apologize about earlier. I'm *super* excited that we're gonna be cellies. This is gonna be awesome!"

Her whole face blooms into joy. She jumps up and squeals, "Ohmigod, I know, right?!"

The following morning, I'm sitting at a table in the cafeteria with Cesar, when a prisoner from my old housing unit sees me. He's seated with a group of inmates adjacent to Cesar and my table. He chuckles at his buddies and calls out to me, "Hey Cox, how's your new cellie, the punk?!"

It feels like half the cafeteria turns to hear my response, and I reply, "Who, Princess? She's awesome!" Immediately there's a cacophony of inmates gasping, "She?" and "Princess?" I instantly add, "Bro, I saw an opportunity to move a punk into my cell and I had to take it; I've been locked up ten years!"

Everyone bursts into laughter.

That's how Miss Martin and I became BFF's.

THE WHOLE TRANSGENDER THING makes me feel very uncomfortable. Like most people, to some degree, initially I think it's a cry for attention or an act, but I quickly learn over time that I'm *absolutely* wrong. No one chooses to subject themselves to a lifetime of ridicule—that's something that chooses you—and if Miss Martin could change her gender-assignment, I know she would. Instead, she does everything in her power to alter her appearance and body to become a female. To fit in. To be the person that she is meant to be.

Eventually, I realize Miss Martin is the mental equivalent of a twelve-year-old middle-class white girl. She is awkward, moody, self-conscious, and cries for no reason—of course the crying may be due to the hormone treatment that the Bureau of Prisons has her on. Regardless, Miss Martin turns out to be one of the coolest people I have met. On top of that, I admire her for embracing her role as a transgender female. In the face of the humiliation most would conceal their true nature, but not her. As a result, despite opening myself up to ridicule by other inmates, out of respect for Miss Martin, I use the female pronoun when referring to her.

If someone has an issue with that, they can go *fuck* themselves.

I'M NOT EVEN PAYING ATTENTION to what is happening in the morning meeting until I hear the peer doing the pull-up say, "Look man, all I know is that it was two o'clock in the morning and I saw four feet underneath the shower stall. That's all I'm sayin'."

What the fuck did I miss, I ask myself. *Did he just say four feet?* I spend so little time mixing with my peers I barely recognize the person accusing the other two program participants of having sex in the showers.

DTS Anderson's eyes almost bulge out of her head and she covers her mouth to stop herself from laughing. DeMille, however, looks confused. She doesn't seem to understand the significance.

"Nah, man," one of the guys snaps, "it ain't like that—" A dozen community members tell him to stick with program's protocol. Still, he continues to try and explain that he was just giving the other guy a haircut. *At 2:00 a.m.!*

Decisively, DeMille blurts out, "Stop talking! Stick with the format."

The two men spend the rest of the mortifying pull-up shaking their heads and shifting in irritation—exhibiting what's known as "bad body language."

The most telling thing about the validity of the pull-up happens later on that day when the guys come up with conflicting versions of why they were in the shower stall together. One inmate says the were giving each other haircuts, while the other states they were praying.

It's a humiliating pull-up, however, it is also, by far, my favorite pull-up to date.

ATTITUDE CHECK

WEDNESDAY, APRIL 18, 2018, I got irritated while sitting in the library. I went there to work, but there were several guys talking loudly. I mentally visualized myself popping each of them in the head with a 9 millimeter. Pop! Pop!! Pop!!!

Which attitude was I struggling with- Humility.

After thinking about the situation, I realized that the inmates didn't comprehend that they were upsetting me. Plus, if I were to execute them—even though it's totally justified—I'm still a felon and I'm not allowed to possess a firearm. That's a three year mandatory minimum!

Which attitude was I demonstrating- Objectivity.

If I continue working on these positive attitudes I will get through the next year without having an altercation.

I'M SITTING IN CONTENT GROUP, listening to a peer complain, the first time I hear DTS Anderson mention that she, like Dr. Smith, has a PhD.

"Really?" questions a peer. Anderson had been at Coleman longer than The Doctor. "So why aren't you running the program?"

"They offered it to me," she replied dismissively, "but I didn't want the responsibility. I enjoy my free time too much."

Intuitively, I know something isn't right. Anderson pronounces education, "edgumacation," and liked, "likeded." I just can't fathom that a woman whom I'd heard tell my peers to, "remesmerize" all eight Criminal Thinking Errors or "leaveout" the program, could have earned a doctorate.

Anderson isn't stupid, she's just "ghetto." I actually like her, but she is clearly envious of Dr. Smith. I mention the absurdity of the lie to Davis—the peer that months earlier had gotten me yanked into the doctor's office because he mistakenly believed I'd written a racist statement. He is now a comp and a unit orderly, however, he still has to attend process group. Davis admits that Anderson had mentioned her PhD to his class as well. I *intentionally* joke that one of us should make an announcement during the morning meeting "that from now on DTS Anderson should be addressed as Dr. Anderson."

I specifically make the statement in the hope Davis will run with the idea . . . and he does.

Days later, in group, Davis declares that he's going to make the announcement the following day. "As an African-American woman," he says to Anderson, "earning a PhD is a big deal."

"Davis," she replies, seemingly nervous, "don't do that. I don't want people callin' me doctor. That's important to Dr. Smith, not me."

"Nah," he retorts, "it's too important—as an African-American woman." Anderson's lips tightened.

After class she takes him aside and orders him not to make the announcement; stating that it would upset Dr. Smith and cause her problems. Davis subsequently confides in me that he could tell she sensed he was taunting her.

Days later, Davis is called into Dr. Smith's office and she asks him why DTS Anderson wants him moved to another process group. "What did you do?"

"Nothing," he replies. He then recalls his suggestion of the morning meeting announcement and grins. "Well, I did suggest that we should all start calling her Dr. Anderson, you know, 'cause of her PhD . . ."

"PhD!" snaps Dr. Smith. "She doesn't have a PhD." Dr. Smith

informed Davis that she'd heard that Anderson had told inmates the lie before. "I'm not sure what her problem is, but it's becoming an issue."

A short time later, during one of Dr. Smith's morning meeting speeches, wherein she states "I have a PhD" half a dozen times, The Doctor shoots DTS Anderson a split-second glance and adds, "I'm the *only* staff member of RDAP that has a PhD." I nearly burst into laughter at the absurdity of it. "None of the drug treatment specialists in *this* program have a PhD."

Davis grins at me from across the sea of prisoners seated between us. He then twists his head around to where Anderson is leaning against the wall and he grins at her. She appears to be caught somewhere between humiliation and rage. Specifically, due to her disdain for me, I get a perverse pleasure at Anderson's discomfort.

Just after lights out (known in RDAP as "quiet time") Miss Martin asks me if I think any of the DTS's could pass the program. "I don't think Dr. Smith could pass the program," I softy retort from my bunk. If we're caught talking after lights out we are subject to being pulled-up. "She's narcissistic—"

"Grandiose," Martin corrects me and whispers, "You've gotta start using the program terms, Cox."

"I don't have to pass." I remind her. "Definitely grandiose. What's with all that 'I have a PhD' shit?" We discuss The Doctor's issue—cut-off and humility—and decide she's most likely overcompensating for something in her childhood. It's either the lack of a parent's affection or being eclipsed by a rival sibling.

"What about Anderson?" Miss Martin grins at me in the dim light emanating from the bathroom. "Aggressive communication, cut-off, humility, super optimism; Anderson would *never* pass, *never*." Miss Martin moves on to DeMille and, simultaneously, we both hiss, "Awfulizing." She adds, "objectivity—due to her bipolar disorder—and negative self-talk . . . cut-off. She's a fuckin' mess."

The other DTS's suffer from a combination of aggressive communication, a lack of caring, mollification, cognitive indolence, and passive aggression. "What about Garcia?" asks Martin. "He could pass."

"Seriously?" I scoff. "He wants to be here less than I do."

This is when I decide to start writing the outline for the story you are currently reading. During our discussions revolving around the bizarre characters running the place and the *Survivor*-like-drama unfolding throughout the day and the insanity of the morning meetings, I mention the idea to Miss Martin.

"Definitely," she hisses.

In a way, I've already been working on the outline. You see upon my arrival at RDAP I was given a calendar and I'd been meticulously detailing the days' events within its pages.

"You have to expose the insanity of this program," whispers Miss Martin. But that's not my motivation.

The truth is, it's a good program that is extremely necessary. I might mock the program and the staff throughout the pages of this book, but the program is crucial. In reality, it should be expanded.

"I see it as a dark comedy."

ATTITUDE CHECK

SATURDAY, APRIL 20, 2018, my cellie was making a sucking noise through her teeth—she's a tooth sucker! I yelled at her to stop it, but she's like a child, so she started doing it even more. This irritated me to no end.

Which attitude was I struggling with- Humility.

After thinking about it, my cellie is basically a twelve-year-old girl and I need to be patient when dealing with children. So, I decide not to give her a serious ass beating for the teeth sucking.

Which attitude was I demonstrating- Humility.

If I continue these positive attitudes I will be able to better deal with my adolescent pain in the ass teeth sucking cellie.

MY EX-WIFE LIKES TO POP IN for the occasional visit. She's remarried with four kids—one from me and three from the new husband, Nick. Despite being in her early forties, Keyla still looks amazing. Mean as a snake, but very attractive.

Keyla glances around at the other inmates that occupy the visitation room. "I kinda like you being here," she says. "I know where you are all of the time, and when I want to talk to you (she points to one of the correctional officers seated behind the desk) I just have one of the guards go get you."

She grins at me. She grins because she's in a position to give me a hard time and I have to sit here and take it. Keyla loves to make me squirm. She loves to remind me of how far I've fallen.

She once tried to get me to admit that I'd stashed millions in offshore accounts. But I've always refused to play the game.

"Do you have anything else to say?"

She looks around the room again, points to several inmates and asks if I know why they're incarcerated. Two of the guys are bank robbers and one is a sex offender.

"Oh my God," she whispers. "But he's so good looking."

I tell Keyla I would introduce her to him, but, I'm pretty sure he's only into preteen girls. "He was selling videos of a couple twelve-year-old girls having sex with each other." I nod to the sex offender and add, "He seems like a nice guy, but I wouldn't let him babysit your kids."

We talk about our son—he's a student at the University of Central Florida. However, the conversation is short.

"So," she says, "you're almost outta here, huh? Where are you planning on living?"

I tell her that I'll figure something out. "I can always rent a room in a boarding house—"

"Boarding house!" snaps Keyla. "Are you serious?" Suddenly, a thought strikes her and she can't help but smirk. "You can always come work for me. I'll even give you a place in Columbus." Keyla owns a ten unit apartment building on Columbus Drive in Tampa, Florida. It's a ramshackle structure located in one of the most crime-ridden areas of the city. She shoots me a satisfied grin and says, "I can always use a good handyman."

I can't take it anymore. "We both know within a year of my release, I'm living in a half a million dollar condo, driving a two hundred thousand dollar sports car, and banging strippers."

"You *sonofabitch*, I know you've got money buried somewhere."

Despite it not being true, the fact that she believes it makes me happy.

Chapter Eight

"I told my psychiatrist that everyone hates me. He said I was being ridiculous—everyone hasn't met me yet."—Rodney Dangerfield

"INMATE COX," bellows Dr. Smith's voice over the unit's public announcement system, "report to The Doctor's office." I step into her office a minute later; Miss Martin is seated in a guest chair, she has her face covered and she's feigning tears.

"Do you want to explain yourself Cox?" asks Dr. Smith. Irritated, she gestures to Miss Martin and snaps, "She's pregnant."

I snap back, "She said she was on the pill!"

Martin bursts into a laugh and Dr. Smith leans back in shock. "My God, Cox," she gasps, "you didn't miss a beat." The Doctor seems impressed.

Martin has been in and out of Dr. Smith's office all day. It appears the two of them are bonding. The Doctor finds Martin's journey through "the transition" fascinating. Martin will later tell me that Dr. Smith seems unusually interested in me. In fact, the joke was entirely The Doctor's idea.

"So, Cox," she asks, "how are you and Miss Martin getting along?"

"Who Kitten? We're down like four flat tires." Dr. Smith smirks, but I can see she expects a more detailed answer. "It's funny because when I used to worry about going to prison and being raped by a six-foot tall black guy, this wasn't what I had in mind."

Both Martin and Dr. Smith laugh.

The Doctor tells me that she has noticed that I spend an unusual amount of time on the computer. "You spend hours on it," she says. "What're you up to?"

I shrug. "I'm working on something."

"Another novel," she snorts. "You're wasting your time." Dr. Smith tells me I should consider enrolling in the culinary arts or horticulture class. "It would be a better use of your time."

My body temperature spikes at the jab. "I don't like to cook and I'm not planning on being a farmer, but I get your point." I inform The Doctor that I understand she wants me to lower my expectation. To humble myself. "I could do that; get a job at FedEx in the warehouse. I'd probably move up to middle management fairly quickly. When it's in my best interest I can be likable." Dr. Smith nods in agreement. "Meet some chick, move in with her and her kids." Dr. Smith nods at the direction I'm headed. "I could maybe teach little league, have a date night, see a movie once a week." The Doctor likes the idea, so, I let it hang in the air and continue, then I drop the hammer. "My fear is Doc, after a year or two I'll get bored and plan a scam—hit Bank of America for a couple million." The optimism slowly slips from Dr. Smith's face and I close with "or worse, I get depressed and stick the barrel of a gun in my mouth and blow my brains all over the kids' picture hanging on the living room wall."

Miss Martin's eyes bulge slightly and the room goes silent. Frustrated, The Doctor takes a cleansing breath and says, "You can go now Cox."

ATTITUDE CHECK

FRIDAY, MAY 4, 2018, I was irritated that Dr. Smith suggested the entire community—which includes me—were pigs. As a result, each group has bathroom cleaning duty for one week.

Which attitude was I struggling with-Humility.

After thinking about it, I decide that some of the guys are pigs and Dr. Smith didn't distinguish between us. She pretty much thinks we are all the same, so there's no reason to be upset.

Which attitude was I demonstrating-Objectivity.

If I continue to work on these positive attitudes I'll be able to deal with the unfairness of group punishment and people talking to me like I'm a dog. Go RDAP!

ALL GROUPS ARE IN A FULL PANIC. It's the middle of the morning meeting and Dr. Smith is on a rampage. She keeps lecturing us in regard to the community being "sick, sick, sick!" She has kicked several people out of the program within the last week and re-phased more than half a dozen others, primarily for not "holding their peers accountable."

Fear permeated the atmosphere. Participants are turning on one another. Guys are cutting one another's throats and the morning meet is the Roman colosseum.

The bloodletting starts on the first Wednesday of the month. Several comps pull-up Musgrove, an elderly dimwitted crack dealer, for not knowing the program material. He is low hanging fruit. Musgrove becomes agitated and confused; he stumbles while trying to recite the interventions he has been assigned. It's pathetic. The comps look so pleased with themselves that it irritates me.

The following day I pull-up the comps for lack of caring. "You guys saw Musgrove struggling," I sneer, while standing above the crowd of prisoners, "but you didn't even try to help him. You guys are so desperate to save your own skins you've lost sight of the program's goals."

My peers nod in agreement, but the confrontation doesn't go over well with the comps. As I'm walking out of the morning meeting, my buddy Cesar hisses, "What're you doing? You're never gonna pass making enemies of the comps."

"Fuck those smug cocksuckers," I retort. Two of my peers walk by and fire finger-pistols from their hips—signifying that I'm a gunslinger. "I'm not trying to pass."

A few days later, I pull-up Jackie Williams, a tall, but thin aggressive black guy who has a habit of walking around the unit singing and pushing people out of his way. I tell him he's not taking his treatment seriously. "You might as well drop out of RDAP and go back to your old unit," I say. A murmur of disapproval rumbles throughout the community and I'm told to stick with the protocol. I take a deep breath and slap Williams with a couple of interventions I know he won't complete. The guy's a fucking idiot.

Word has gotten around that one of the sex offenders in the program, Daniel Selman, caught Joseph Williamson, a white trash methamphetamine trafficker, paying another inmate—a known bookie and drug dealer—with a bag of commissary. It's a total violation of RDAP principles.

The worst part is that Williamson—who's hooked on Suboxone (a synthetic version of heroin)—is within days of graduating the program. If he's pulled-up for even the smallest infraction at this late date, The Doctor will toss him out of the program and claw back his year.

Unfortunately, minutes after Selman "confront and levels" with Williamson regarding the incident, Williamson corners Selman in his cell. He tells Selman if he pulls him up, Williamson will kill him. "I'll beat you to death in your sleep you fuckin' pervert!"

Selman gets so freaked out by the veracity of Williamson's threat he resolves not to follow through with the pull-up—another violation of the RDAP principals. Guerriero, however, is now considering pulling-up Selman for enabling Williamson. "He obviously doesn't care about his treatment."

"Jesus Christ, bro!" I gasp. We're sitting at one of the hundred-plus chipped formica-tables in the cafeteria. I'm wavering between the entertainment value the confrontation would bring me and seeing these two idiots get kicked out of the program, thrown into the (SHU) Segregated Housing Unit (otherwise known as "the hole"), and shipped to separate prisons. "Just let the guy graduate."

"Are you crazy, do you have any idea how much this helps me?" Unlike my own narcissism, Guerriero's manifests itself in condescension. He's managed to get himself pulled-up over a dozen times within the first phase as well as alienated himself from his peers and pissed off nearly all of the staff. "I can knock off both these two idiots."

I shake my head. I can't help but recognize how *Survivor*

this is. "Just let 'em graduate."

"The problem is, you know that I know, so does Padula, Vitale, and a couple other guys," he admits. "If I don't say anything I could get pulled-up for enabling." He's right of course. I've seen it happen many times.

The morning meeting and graduation comes and go; Guerriero says nothing.

THE NIGHT BEFORE CESAR GRADUATES, May 14, 2018, he steps into my cell. He's scheduled to leave for the Miami halfway house directly after the ceremony.

"Listen," he says, while taking off his wristwatch. "I know you need a watch." Over a week ago, my Ironman timepiece had stopped working, and, because commissary watches are so expensive, I had decided to go without. Cesar hands me his watch and ads, "You know this is my son's watch."

Cesar once confided in me that he planned on giving the watch to his son for his eighteenth birthday. He wanted him to know that he'd once made a mistake that cost him several years of his life. That our decisions have consequences. I love that he wants his darkest moment to be an example to his son.

"I can't take the watch," I say. "What if something happens?"

"Take the watch," he says. "Don't be an asshole, just mail it to me as soon as you get out."

I'M BANGING OUT EDITS when Dr. Smith calls my name over the PA system. She has a direct line of site to the unit's bank of computers. I wheel around and she motions me into her office.

Once seated she states, "Other than your mother and your ex-wife, you barely call anyone." *Fuck!* I tell myself, *She's been going through my phone records.* "You hardly email anyone either." *Fuck! She's been reading my emails.* She flips open a document on her desk—my Pre-Sentence Investigation Report. "Your PSI says you have a son . . ." *This is bad,* I admit to myself. The last thing I want is Dr. Smith taking an interest in me. She's easily got me by ten IQ points and a degree in psychology. "Do you ever talk to him?"

"I, I've, I've talked to him," I stammer out. The walls are starting to close in and I instinctively glance at the door.

"You're not leaving Cox." She lets the statement hang in the air and says, "Based on your PSI, your response to confrontation is to flee." I was, in fact, on the run from federal law enforcement for three years. For two of those years, I was number one on the Secret Service's most wanted list. However, I have no issue with confrontation. It's the fear of the unknown that causes me extreme anxiety. Consequences are what I fear. "When was the last time you spoke to him, Cassio?"

Fuck! Fuck! Fuck! "Maybe two years ago," I admit. "He doesn't want anything to do with me." Dr. Smith asks why and I remind her that I abandoned him at the age of five to avoid the FBI and the Secret Service as well as my inevitable incarceration. "He's got a valid reason to hate me."

I can feel my typical coarse veneer softening at the thought of him. At the thought of what I'd put him through.

"What about his mother, Keyla, she visits you pretty regularly," notes Dr. Smith, "she's never brought him to see you?" I explain that Cass is nineteen years old, a man. She can't force him to come. "Not now, but when he was a boy she could have brought him. She could have made him—"

"Maybe, but I gave up the right to second guess her the moment I took off." In fact, my ex-wife made sure that Cass was immersed in my family. He regularly spent time with my parents, and his uncles, aunts, and his cousins. He attended all of the Cox's family celebrations. She did such an amazing job of it, that Keyla's children from her second marriage think my mother is their grandmother.

Heat rushes into my face and my throat tightens when I say, "No, Keyla's a good person. I fucked up." My nose is running and my eyes start to burn. I glance at the door again as the tears roll down my face. "She made the choice she thought was best."

Dr. Smith tells me she's impressed that I won't say anything negative about my ex-wife. However, she, The Doctor, feels Keyla could have done more to help mend Cassio's and my relationship. Tears are dripping from my nose. The air is hot and humid like a sauna.

I can see that Dr. Smith is moved by my rare show of emotion. So, hoping for some leeway, I ask her if I can leave. I tell her I want to go back to my cell. "Cox, don't you think you should deal with this?"

"I am dealing with it." I explain that I'd mentally placed the idea of my son in a box and I'd place that box on a shelf in the back of my mind. I know that it's there, but I don't focus on it or discuss it. "I only get upset when I think about him—"

"That's not dealing with it," she sighs; and explains that I need to talk about my son now, so that someday, when he eventually decides to speak with me, I can discuss the issue without becoming overly emotional.

Dr. Smith stares at me as I gaze at the floor. I'm desperate to stop the tears. To close the box. I'm so embarrassed it hurts. A minute goes by and then two. The room feels tight. Finally, she whispers, "Cox, if you'd just talk about—"

"Can I please leave Dr. Smith?" I gasp. "Please, please, can I just leave, *pleeease*?"

Her eyes are filled with sympathy and she answers, "For now."

CURRENTLY, I'M WORKING on Vitale's story. It turns out that the circumstances surrounding the handsome ex-stock broker's case are fascinating; involving multiple multi-million dollar scams interwoven with two murders. His tale of pump and dump schemes is filled with strippers and Lambos.

Using the state and federal freedom of information acts, I order the documents relative to his case and wait.

I know that Vitale's story will be my last. *It doesn't matter,* I tell myself. *I'll keep in touch with a few guys and they'll feed me stories.* But it won't be the same as sitting with my subjects. Looking into their eyes and reading them. It won't be the same over the phone or email.

ATTITUDE CHECK

FRIDAY, MAY 19, 2018, I was waiting in the cafeteria line and there were several inmates standing behind me screaming. I was so irritated I began mentally visualizing myself striking each of them in the head with a baseball bat. I could almost hear the crunch of their skulls.

Which attitude was I struggling with- Humility

Looking back on the incident, I realize that I was allowing myself to get upset by them, when they were simply having a conversation. It's not their fault that they are ill-mannered idiots that were raised poorly by what I can only imagine were uncultured trash.

Which attitude was I demonstrating- Open mindedness and humility.

If I continue to work on applying these positive attitude checks I will learn to cope with the stress of being surrounded by scumbags. Go RDAP!

Chapter Nine

"In a mad world, only the mad are sane."—Akira Kurosawa

MCKINNON STANDS UP immediately when Padula calls his name. A dead-ringer for a twenty-five-year-old Dwayne "The Rock" Johnson, at six-foot six-inches, McKinnon towers over the other RDAP participants. The gang member—doing time for a drug conspiracy out of Hawaii—had been on his best behavior, but this morning my intuition tells me something is wrong.

McKinnon's mother is dying of cancer and if he doesn't make the next graduating class, he's let it be known he fears he'll never see her alive.

Unfortunately, Padula had caught him smoking K2 in the restroom a few nights earlier. He'd confront and leveled with McKinnon, but the gang member denied it. Understand, Padula is a large man, however, he's also a grey haired fiftyish CEO-type whose only crime was cheating on his taxes.

McKinnon steps out of the row of seated prisoners to face his accuser. Staring into McKinnon's eyes, Padula describes the incident and McKinnon's struggles. Everything seems fine, but when the seasoned-CEO states, "The damaging consequences of your actions are—" McKinnon bolts forward, fists clinched and barks, "I've got you're *damaging consequences* motherfucker!"

Padula pivots to his right, but the blow catches him on the shoulder and spins him around. The entire room leaps to their feet and a dozen prisoners rush McKinnon. Immediately, the DTS's push the body alarms on their radios. In the struggle to restrain McKinnon, the gang member takes a swing at Guerriero.

Seconds later the room is engulfed by correctional officers and we're hastily ordered to return to our cells.

While the staff is questioned about the fight by investigators with the prison's Special Investigations Service, we're confined to our cells. This takes most of the day.

Shortly after dinner, I'm regaling Pete and a guy named Donovan Davis with a blow-by-blow account of the morning meeting. Donovan is a large Jamaican who's locked up for running a Ponzi scheme. He loves to laugh. The three of us are cracking up when Bill Clark * approached the table. Clark, a typically grumpy sex offender in his mid-sixties, is doing twenty years for having sex with a seventeen-year-old on film, which constitutes production of child pornography.

* Name has been changed.

He looks perplexed. Clark and I were cellies for a while and I have a soft spot for him, so, I ask if anything is wrong. "You're not gonna fuckin' believe this," he announces to the table; then proceeds to tell us that the correctional officer working his unit —an older white haired Andy Griffith-type—called him into his office and sparked up a conversation with him. During the discussion Clark realized the officer was checking him out and he got a strong homosexual-vibe from the guy. He asked Clark if he worked out, told him he was in good shape, and asked him how much time he'd done. "Then, outta the fuckin' blue, that queen asked me if I was gay—"

"What the fuck!" I snap. "Are you serious?"

Clark told the officer he wasn't gay and, feeling uncomfortable, asked to be excused, but the officer kept fishing. "That motherfucking fag said, 'You know, if you're locked up and you have sex with another man, it doesn't make you gay.' I told him, 'Yeah, it does,' and I left."

The entire table burst into laughter and Pete gasps, "Don't be so hasty, you've got a lot of time; this could be your get outta jail free card." As a ward of the Bureau of Prisons, even a consensual relationship between an officer and an inmate is considered rape under federal law. "Start keeping a record. You need to go back to the unit and document the encounter in the computer—"

"Yeah," I cut in, "if he lights some candles and puts on some soft music, who knows, you might get into it." The table erupts into laughter again and Donovan adds, "It doesn't have to be penetration, you could just give him a reach around."

"I'm not doin' that," grunts Clark. "There's something wrong with you fuckers!"

He turns to walk away and I blurt out, "We're just saying... keep the sample, that's all."

Subsequently, I learn that the officer in question has, over the years, had several complaints filed against him by inmates, ranging from sexual advances to fondling prisoners during pat downs. However, much like the Catholic Church, instead of firing the officer the BOP simply reassigned him to another prison and buried the complaints.

UNDER THE DOCTOR AND DTS'S GUIDANCE, more and more of the members of my group are "drinking the Kool- Aid." Primarily this is done through the "community as a method" model. Much like Jonestown, our community is isolated and thoroughly supervised both externally and internally.

The Jonestown Compound was founded in November 1978 by Jim Jones, an American preacher turned cult leader. Specifically, he located the facility in the remote country of Guiana, Africa. Watched by Jones' armed security and inundated by his dogma the majority of his nine hundred-plus subjects accepted his testament. In fact, his subjects had been so thoroughly brainwashed, when things eventually began to go wrong and it appeared that Jones was losing control he ordered his followers to drink the beverage, Flavored Aide. Unfortunately, for his subjects the drink was laced with chloral hydrate and cyanide.

Most drank the beverage willingly, but some resisted and were forced by Jones' guards to consume the poisonous cocktail. Over nine hundred members perished.

Expectedly, due to the constant lectures by Dr. Smith, the

DTS run classes, the senior-peer supervised workshops as well as the ever increasing homework assignments, participants are buying into the RDAP doctrine at a mind-blowing rate. However, in my opinion, the most effective tool in the program's arsenal is the constant informing of the smallest infraction by its participants. Thus, keeping virtually everyone in line.

The total immersion in the program's philosophy is like nothing I've ever experienced.

ATTITUDE CHECK

THURSDAY, MAY 31, 2018, my cellie has been giving me dirty looks and acting bitchy— it's like being locked up with my ex-wife! This "chick" needs to cut back on the hormone therapy. She's going batshit crazy.

Which attitude was I struggling with-Objectivity.

Later she explained that due to the supplemental hormones she takes, she gets cramps and mood swings. This makes her irritable. Now I feel a little bit bad for my crazy tranny cellie. God only knows what's going on inside of her head.

Which attitude was I demonstrating-Open mindedness.

If I continue these positive attitudes I will learn to alter my flawed way of thinking.

"COX, COME TO THE DOCTOR'S OFFICE," bellows Dr. Smith over the unit's speakers. I'd been trying to sit at the one computer outside her office's line of sight, but The Doctor noticed me as she came in from lunch.

Dr. Smith motions to a guest chair as I enter the room. My PSI is sitting on her desk. I tell her I'm in the middle of something and she replies, "Sit down." Like an obedient pet, I obey. "How much time do you spend on the computer?"

"Maybe an hour a day," I answer and Dr. Smith scoffs. I admit, "Maybe two?"

"You're on it for four or five hours a day; I want you to start keeping a log and turn it into me at the end of the week." Specifically, Dr. Smith feels the log will help me understand that I'm spending too much time on my "urban novels" and not enough time on my emotional issues. "Are you still taking the antidepressants?"

Prior to my incarceration I'd been prescribed Paxil and Xanax for depression and anxiety—panic attacks, specifically. But the BOP refused to give me Xanax—a controlled substance—and they switched me from Paxil to a succession of cheaper antidepressants that simply didn't work.

"No, ma'am, I'm dealing with it on my own."

"Is it in a box on a shelf—"

"No, I just figured out the cycle and I talk myself through it."

"Tell me about the cycle," she says, and I look at the door. "The computer's not going anywhere."

I take a deep cleansing breathe and admit, "The morning is the worst." Typically, when I wake up around 5:00 a.m., my first thought is of dental floss. "How much dental floss would I have to buy to make a rope strong enough to hang myself from the bar over the handicap stall?" I tell myself, *It's an irrational thought, influenced by a lack of serotonin.* "It takes about five minutes to convince myself that coffee will fix it ... and I crawl outta bed."

Dr. Smith looks concerned, but I keep talking.

"By nine or ten I'm in the library, writing, and I start to feel I can make it to commissary day."

"For the dental floss?"

"For the dental floss," I admit. "But by lunch I've spoken to Pete and I decide I'd miss him too much and the dental-floss is a bad idea. A pathetic idea. A stupid idea ..." Then the serotonin kicks in. By roughly 2:00 p.m. I began thinking, *My life isn't that bad.* By 5:00 p.m., I'm feeling good. "I start thinking how lucky I am to be in a prison with such great characters and amazing stories. By seven I'm telling myself, I'm getting outta here, I'm gonna option the film rights to over a dozen stories to Hollywood and make millions!" I chuckle at the absurdity of the fantasy and continue, "By lights out I see myself on the cover of *Rolling Stone* magazine holding an Academy Award and I pass out ... and at five the next morning I wake up and wonder, *How much dental-floss am I gonna need.*"

There's a long silence between us; eventually Dr. Smith

asks, "How long has this been going on?"

"Not long," I confess. "About a decade."

"WHY WOULD YOU TELL HER that?" asks Guerriero. It's 7:00 a.m. and we're eating breakfast—oatmeal and hardboiled eggs—in the cafeteria. I can never get the shell off of the fucking eggs. "She could've had you locked up, put on suicide watch."

"She's not gonna do that." Dr. Smith could have had me held for observation, but I knew she wouldn't. Narcissists hardly ever kill themselves. "Unlike you," I chuckle, "she likes me."

"She would have had them strip me naked and thrown in observation for sure."

The Doctor can't stand Guerriero. Other than myself, Padula, and Vitale, nearly everyone in RDAP despises him. He's exceedingly arrogant, condescending, and manipulative. He's been pulled-up half a dozen times within the last thirty days.

"You know," I say, "it's a fuckin' miracle you haven't been kicked out yet."

Chapter Ten

"My wish is that you may be loved to the point of madness."—Andre Breton

MISS MARTIN HAS BEEN SULKING all day. I ask her a few times if everything is okay; she mumbles something about hormones and I figure it's none of my business. However, that night I'm lying in my bunk when she hisses, "Cox! Cox! You awake?"

"Fuck," I grumble. "I am now." She's seated on the side of her bed wiping tears out of her eyes. "Christ, what'd he do now? Miss Martin's boyfriend, Jovonise Williams, is a constant cause of drama. This isn't the first time I've been woken up to comfort her. It happens once, sometimes twice, a week.

"We, we, we broke up," she sniffs. "He said he doesn't wanna be with me on the street."

"The guy's a fuckin' retard, you know that." Jovonise is a low level drug dealer with his prison GED and Martin was one year away from her Bachelor of Science when she was picked up on a white collar case. "He's a tatted-wannabe-thug and you're a smart, attractive chick with everything in the world going for you. On the street you wouldn't want anything to do with that fucking scumbag." The fact that I'm in a prison, consoling a transgender-female at midnight, is not lost on me. *I can't believe I'm having this conversation*, I tell myself. *This is fucking insanity.*

"If I'm so great," she whimpers, "then why doesn't he want me?"

"I have no idea." In truth, much like the puppet-maker Geppetto, Jovonise wants a *real* girl; and outside of the prison's walls he won't need a blue fairy to get one. "You can do better."

WE CAN HEAR ADRIAN JOHNSON yelling from down the hall. He'd been called into Counselor Thomas' office minutes earlier. Thomas, an avid fitness buff, whom the inmates and staff call "Pretty Ricky," due to his jerry-curled hair and an almost imperceptible amount of foundation, a nickname he loathes. He'd been calling guys in all morning to discuss raising their FRP payments and something had gone wrong.

"Motherfucker, I'm a grown ass man!" Johnson is a drug dealer with an anger management problem. As it turns out, when Pretty Ricky told Johnson he was going to have to start paying more FRP every month, Johnson stated that he couldn't afford to pay more. Pretty Ricky then pulled-up his commissary receipts and started to read off all of the things he felt Johnson was wasting his money on—potato chips, Snickers bars, Honey Buns, *et cetera*. He then suggested Johnson should think of this as an opportunity to lose some weight. That's when Johnson lost his temper.

I look up just in time to see an infuriated Johnson storm into Dr. Smith's office and demand to sign out of the program.

When I return from lunch two hours later, I see Johnson in his cell busily writing in his RDAP workbook. I ask him when Dr. Smith is moving him back to his old housing unit. "She ain't," he admits, seeming slightly embarrassed. "She talked me into stayin' . . . and I had to apologize to that pretty motherfucker too."

"Why not just quit?"

He shrugs. "A lot of what she says makes sense," he admits. "The thing is Cox . . . I need the program."

Counselor Thomas calls me to his office the next day. He points to his computer screen and says, "You're on FRP refusal. You can't be in the program if you're on FRP refusal."

"Yeah," I retort, "I've been meaning to talk to you about that."

Thomas fancies himself a tough guy. In reality, he is a meticulously groomed African-American metrosexual that has the sleeves of his uniforms altered to fit tight to his biceps.

As Thomas explains why he believes I should pay twenty-five dollars a month—far less than the one hundred dollars Counselor Thompson had stuck me with—I can't help but notice he's wearing foundation and the line encircling his eyes seems a little too dark.

Regardless, Pretty Ricky hooks me up with a reasonable FRP payment and even agrees to put the commencement date off for several months. I'm so thrilled with the payment, I don't even care that this guy is wearing eyeliner.

ATTITUDE CHECK

FRIDAY, JUNE 22, 2018, I had a conversation with a guy regarding fraud. I enjoyed the subject so much that I thought about it all day and night—it made me feel hopeful.

Which attitude was I struggling with-Objectivity.

After thinking about the conversation and the euphoric affect it had on me, I realized that it was not a constructive conversation and I shouldn't talk about fraud in the future.

Which attitude was I demonstrating-Objectivity.

If I continue to work on these positive attitudes, I will eventually alter my behavior, and maybe I'll have a shot at a normal life on the streets.

THE ENTIRE RDAP STAFF was seated in Dr. Smith's office, when myself and a couple of my peers—guys chosen by me for support—sat facing the panel. The Doctor and her colleagues had been randomly teaming the programs' participants for the last several days—re-phasing some and even throwing a couple of guys out.

Each DTS gives a glowing assessment of me, including Anderson. I have to cover my face to shield a grin when she informs Dr. Smith, "Mr. Cox has a firm understanding of the material. He participates and gives honest feedback."

The truth is, I've only briefly looked over the material; and I only did that because a senior-peer who was assigned to me, (known as a "big brother"), is terrified that my group will be tested on the material any day now. I will of course fail miserably and he will be blamed (or "held accountable.") Still, I know virtually nothing. If asked, I couldn't name the attitudes of change, the criminal thinking patterns, the thinking errors or any of the other stuff I'm supposed to know by this point. Damn sure couldn't recite the programs philosophy.

As my peers praise my progress, Dr. Smith just stares at me. She knows it's a farce. She cuts them off. "Tell me about your criminal thinking Cox; any progress there?"

I think about lying to her, but there's no benefit to it. I take a deep breath and say, "A couple day ago, I was talking to a guy in the chow hall about what's called 'the drop;' it's a scam where you fraudulently claim other people's tax refunds." I explain that it's become an issue for the IRS and they're implementing security measures to try and stop this fraud. "We talked for around twenty minutes about the IRS's procedures and . . . I spent the rest of the day thinking about how to get around them." Specifically, I spoke with a CPA doing time for money laundering and two other inmates locked up for tax fraud. "Not only do I think I found a way to circumvent the new procedures, but I also found a way to improve on the scam and maximize the yield."

One of my peers hisses through his teeth, "Jesus Christ, Cox, what're you doing?" Dr. Smith shushes him and asks me to continue.

"That's pretty much it," I admit. "By the end of the day I was so jacked-up on adrenaline my hands were shaking." Dr. Smith and I lock eyes for a second, and I close with, "It's the best I've felt in weeks."

"SO, HOW MUCH IS ONE OF THOSE THINGS?" I ask. Miss Martin and I are discussing the surgeries she's planning to get upon her release and the associated cost.

"They're expensive Cox." She tells me that the price of the, "boobs, ass cheek, and hips are only around ten thousand, but the V . . . the V is between twenty to thirty grand."

"Fuck!" I gasp. "That's nuts." Miss Martin thinks about the surgeries all of the time. She's got several books on the subject and one massive instruction manual on the transitioning. I ask what she plans on doing with the left overs. "You gonna keep your junk in a jar of formaldehyde; maybe display the nuts and bolt on a shelf in your apartment or—"

"No!" She bursts into laugher at the thought; then turns serious. Miss Martin tells me she doesn't want to keep anything as a memento. She wants the entire package gone. Permanently disposed of. "This thing's caused me nothing but problems."

Transitioning from a male to female is not an easy thing. There are psychology appointments, hormone replacement therapy, laser hair removal, and the most invasive and costly being sexual reassignment surgery.

"Vaginoplasty's expensive," Miss Martin informs me. "A vagina is expensive."

That has certainly been my experience. "It's expensive," I say, "because it's the money maker."

HE FIXED A MICROWAVE, that was all the guy had done and Dr. Smith kicked him out of the program.

Microwaves are a big problem at Coleman. The budget gets smaller every year; therefore, the prison doesn't have the resources (or refuses to designate them) to replace the aging microwaves. Instead, despite an institution policy prohibiting prisoners from working on the microwaves, the inmates are constantly taking it upon themselves to repair the devices. In particular, there is this little sex offender, Roger Clark *, that can fix pretty much anything. Clark is so adept at repairs that, when the microwave broke in the office in the B-3 housing unit, the correctional officer asked him to fix it. Since inmates aren't allowed to disobey a direct order from an officer, Clark fixed the microwave.

* Name has been changed.

Days later, The Doctor called Clark into her office and confronted him with the violation of the institution policy. She didn't care that he'd been given an order by an officer; she just told him to pack his stuff and moved him back to his old housing unit.

At times, Dr. Smith can be unreasonable like that. Here's the thing, three months later Clark re-applied to the program and she moved him right back in.

I mention this because I'm sitting in the library working on the outline for the very book you're reading when Michael Sayer—a peer I almost never talk too—slips into a chair across from me. "You're writing a book about the program," he asks, "right?"

"A synopsis for sure," I reply, "maybe a book."

He tells me that he just left Dr. Smith's office. "This morning I walked in on Clark and Sawyer in the backroom." Sawyer is not only the head orderly and comp, he's also Dr. Smith's main informant. Everyone despises him. "That snitch Sawyer, was keeping lookout, while Clark worked on that microwave that went down the other day."

"Oh shit," I hiss. I assume that Sayer is planning on pulling-up both Sawyer and Clark. I can't imagine him not taking the opportunity to gut Sawyer like a fish in front the community. I would. "You gonna pull him up, crack him in the head?"

"Nah," Sayer glances around the library, makes sure no one is close enough to hear him, and he says, "Dr. Smith called me into her office and asked me to look the other way." The Doctor had specifically divulged that she'd felt bad that the guys in the unit only had one microwave. Therefore, she personally asked Clark to repair the second nonfunctioning microwave. She was just trying to look out for them. "Then she told me that I was graduating soon and she wouldn't want this to become an issue for me." Sayer arches an eyebrow at The Doctor's veiled threat and he grins at the dichotomy. "She's so fucking manipulative, she kicked that little cho-mo (child molester) out for the same fuckin' thing. She's ah... What's that word, when you say one thing and—"

"Hypocrite."

"Right," he snaps. "She's a hypocrite."

ATTITUDE CHECK

SATURDAY, JULY 8, 2018, my cellie said I was an out of shape old white man, and if I didn't start working out I would never get a hot young girlfriend when I get out of prison. That pissed me off to the point I began thinking about waiting until she fell asleep, placing a pillow over her head and yelling, "Don't fight it! Go into the light! Go into the light!"

Which attitude was I struggling with-Humility.

After thinking about it, I do want a hot young girlfriend, so, I probably should start working out. My cellie is actually right... Thank God I didn't smother her.

Which attitude was I demonstrating-Open mindedness.

If I continue to be open minded about my faults I can work on improving them. If that happens then I will get that hot young girlfriend I totally deserve. Go RDAP!

I CATCH MY RDAP UNIT COUNSELOR, Counselor Hammette, in the hallway and I ask him if the management variable has been placed on me? "Not yet Cox," he replies. "But don't worry about it, you can't be moved as long as you're in the program."

"Yeah, I know." Hammette is cool. He's a straight-shooter-paycheck-employee. He's not trying to give the inmates a hard time. So, I feel comfortable informing him that, "I may be dropping out and I just wanna know that the management variable is in place *before* that happens."

His grin tells me he understands. "It'll probably be another week or two." He replies. "I'll let you know."

"THE COMMUNITY IS SICK," Dr. Smith informs us, her would-be disciples. Her gaze passes over the mass of one hundred and fifty "believers." Each RDAP member sits up taut as her eyes pass over them. Many nod their heads in agreement. "There's a cancer growing inside the community and something has to be done."

I've heard the speech before. According to Tamayo, Dr. Smith's clerk, she's been giving The Community is Sick speech the whole time he's been in the RDAP Unit—nearly four years.

She needs some new material, I tell myself. My attention begins to drift when I hear The Doctor reference her PhD. Miss Martin and I make eye contact from across the room and we almost burst into laughter. Today, however, Dr. Smith only mentions her doctoral twice. *That's a shame,* I think, *I've counted as many as eight.*

Shortly after the speech, she begins purging what I can only assume she considered cancerous members. Throughout the week she ejects and re-phases a dozen inmates.

IT'S JULY 12, 2019, and Guerriero is distraught. An hour earlier, during his team, Dr. Smith re-phased him. He's no longer allowed to hang out with Padula or Vitale—the narcissists. She feels they're a bad influence on one another, but she didn't mention me. "How have you not been re-phased?" asks Guerriero. "You don't do anything. You never study. You don't know the material."

"I don't go to my AA meetings or those fucking workshops either," I add with a chuckle. I know it's killing Guerriero. Dr. Smith is toying with him, and, from his perspective, she's taking it easy on me. He doesn't know about our talks, nor does he know how emotionally damaged I am.

"WHAT THE FUCK IS THAT BITCH DOIN' to you Cox?" asks Miss Martin when I step in to our cell. I'd spent the last hour in Dr. Smith's office. I thought I looked composed, but my eyes are bloodshot and puffy. My face is red. "I'm gonna talk to her—"

"No," I say. "You'll just make it worse."

"What does she expect from you?" Specifically, Dr. Smith now wants me to start writing a letter per week to my son. When I told her I couldn't do it, she informed me that if I didn't produce a letter on my own, she would have me sit in her office all day until I wrote them. The thought of sitting inside of that oppressive little box, suffocating from claustrophobia, causes me to inhale deeply. I collapse onto my bed and admit, "She said it wasn't up for debate."

Miss Martin sits across from me and timidly asks, "Can, can you write them?"

I'm so emotionally drained, so physically exhausted all I can think about is sleep. "I can't write them without getting upset." Any prolonged internal or external discussion related to my son immediately brings tears to my eyes. Martin know this. I whisper, "I can't stand her."

"I know you don't wanna hear this, but she wants you to face this. She wants you to get better." Miss Martin offers to write the letters for me. "She'll never know."

I wipe the saline off of my face and say, "No, I'll do it. I'll do it."

"WHEN ARE YOU COMING HOME?" asks my mom during our visit. I'm seated facing her. The room is full, but it's not too loud. There are no kids running around screaming. The wheelchair makes her look small and frail. Her caregiver is seated across the room reading her bible. "Next month?"

"No, mom," I say. I'm still waiting for the BOP to process my halfway house request. It's a long process and the date is tenuous. "Probably in late-December, but it might be in January."

She tells me that she and her caregiver are going to visit my father at the cemetery on their way home. "Just for a few minutes," she says. "He doesn't talk much."

I shake my head in disapproval and she grins.

Chapter Eleven

"Sometimes I sit quietly and I wonder why I am not in a mental asylum. Then I look around at everyone and realize ... maybe I already am."—Edgar Allen Poe

THERE ARE NO PULL-UPS and it's a problem. For the third time, the inmate facilitator asks, "Does anyone have a pull-up?" and, still, no one raises their hand.

It's 8:10 a.m. He shrugs it off and moves on to the next order of business when DTS DeMille stops him. She rushes out of the room and a minute later Dr. Smith strolls in looking perplexed. She asks, "Are there any pull-ups?" but no one raises their hand. She nods, asks the facilitators to take their chairs. "Everyone is to remain in your seat until you're given instructions." Subsequently, she and all of the DTS's exit the room.

Fifteen minutes later many of the guys start talking among themselves. Suddenly, DeMille steps into the room and yells at everyone to remain quiet. "No talking! No reading or writing! Dr. Smith said to sit there and be *quiet!*"

Like scolded children, the entire room goes silent. The minutes start ticking away and the plastic chair I'm seated on becomes less and less accommodating with each passing second. Within thirty minutes some of the inmates begin to look panicked. Nature is calling, but they're too scared to risk walking to the restroom. Eventually, a senior participant asks DeMille for permission and a dozen prisoners run out of the room.

We sit in the ever increasing unpleasantness of the large room. Waiting and waiting. My left leg is falling asleep. I begin to make a note of the punishment in my RDAP calendar, but another peer shakes his head in condemnation. I place the pen back in my datebook and wait. I shift from one ass cheek to the other in an attempt to get comfortable.

At a quarter after nine it becomes obvious that we aren't going to be released for our classes. Instead, Dr. Smith keeps us seated. Another two hours goes by until DTS DeMille storms in and tells us that we can go to lunch.

My ass is killing me.

For the entire day, the unit is in turmoil. The participants are grumbling their anger at having to sit for hours on end. Guys are quoting BOP policy which states humiliation cannot be used as a form of punishment, but I know, come the following morning, there will be two dozen prisoners ready and waiting with pull-ups.

I laugh about it with Miss Martin. "Shit," I confide, "if none of these idiots has a pull-up I'm gonna pull-up five or six guys."

"Who?" she giggles. I name four guys I've caught sleeping in the library within the last week. Plus, there's Robinson, a skinny crackhead in our group that refuses to take a shower, and Vitale, he's been high on Suboxone—a synthetic opioid, prescribed to help relieve symptoms of heroin withdrawal—for the last two months. "Cox," Martin gasps, "Vitale's a friend of yours—"

"Right," I laugh, "and as a friend, I'm gonna hold him accountable—" Martin rears back in disgust. "What?!" I snap. "You're trying to make me feel bad, is that it? Listen *Princess*, I'm a sociopath, you can't make me feel bad." I inform her that I have no intention of "sitting in that hard-ass-fuckin' chair for another three and a half hours ... *Fuck!* I might pull *you* up."

"Don't say that Cox," she whimpers. "You're gonna make me cry."

I can't believe this is my life, I tell myself. *I gotta get outta this fucking unit.*

ATTITUDE CHECK

ON, FRIDAY, JULY 20, 2018, I was sitting in the morning meeting when the pull-up portion arrived, however, there were no pull-ups. Dr. Smith got upset and stopped the meeting.

Instead of moving forward, she decided to have us sit quietly like scolded children for three hours. It was a sad sad power move meant to humiliate the entire community. In the end I believe it made Dr. Smith look pathetic and I feel bad for her.

Which attitude was I struggling with- Caring.

After thinking about it, maybe I don't understand what Dr. Smith's motives are. However, that's unlikely. Regardless, she does keep telling us she's got a PhD, over and over and over again. So, maybe there's something behind her madness that I don't understand. I'm just a scumbag criminal, that happens to have an IQ of 140. What do I know?

Which attitude was I demonstrating- Open mindedness.

If I continue thinking in a positive way I will be a more obedient, moldable person upon my release. Like a lamb to the slaughter, I will blindly follow authority like a good citizen. Go RDAP!

THE NEXT MORNING, seated in the pool of participants, the atmosphere is tense. Everything is running like clockwork, however, as the meeting facilitator asks, "Are there any pull-ups," Dr. Smith marches into the room and scowls at the group. She turns and orders the facilitator to take his seat; then tells everyone to remain in our chairs "Until instructed otherwise."

Fuck! I scream internally. *I can't believe this is happening, again.*

Thirty minutes into our punishment I realize the DTS's aren't coming back to resume the meeting and we are most likely down for the duration of the program day, so, I pull out my calendar and I start making notes. I'm jotting down how bad my ass hurts when one of my peers reminds me that we were specifically told not to do any reading *or* writing. I lean toward him and whisper, "Pull me up, bro. I'll take the hit."

We are released at 11:15 a.m. for lunch.

The unit is in an uproar throughout the entire weekend. There are rumors that Dr. Smith is thinking about scrapping the program's current groups and starting over. "It's been done before," says one panicked participant. "I heard they shut the program down in Pensacola for six months." Another guy insisted that she was planning "a massive Stalin-style purge." Still, someone else swears that The Doctor is planning a mass "testing of the entire unit on the material."

One thing is certain, the RDAP participants are one hundred percent focused on their studies and watching one another for the smallest infraction.

Monday morning, July 23, 2018, once again, when the facilitator gets to the pull-ups Dr. Smith walks in and stops the meeting. Sure enough, The Doctor tells us to remain seated and she leaves. *Unfuckingbelievable!*

Nearly three hours later, Dr. Smith walks back into the morning meeting. She surveys the group of suitably humiliated inmates, clears her throat, and inquires, "Can anyone tell me why I cancelled the morning meeting and all of the classes, just to have you sit and reflect?"

Several eager inmates' hands shot into the air. All of their answers incorporate some aspect of accountability, but Dr. Smith isn't satisfied with their answers. "You guys," she gripes, "It's more than just accountability, it's caring and..." Honestly, I couldn't tell you what else she said. I can report that she went on and on for twenty minutes and ended with "Does everyone understand?"

Dozens of the participants nod their understanding and I think, *Wouldn't it be funny if someone said, No. It would be great for the book. Of course, no one would dare, they all have too much to lose ... but I don't.*

As Dr. Smith turns to leave, I raise my hand high. She scrunches her brow and asks, "Mr. Cox?"

I stand and say, "I don't understand." She looks perplexed, dumbfounded really. So, I clarify my statement. "You asked if everyone understood, and I don't. I didn't learn anything Dr. Smith . . ." I feel my resolve ebbing, then, suddenly, I get a surge of adrenaline and I bark, "You know what I learned by sitting in these hard ass plastic chair—that I *know* the staff ain't sitting in—is that, after about an hour, my ass hurts." Several of the participants hiss at me to calm down and stick with the format, but there is no format for calling the RDAP coordinator on her bullshit. "I learned that my ass hurts and you were pissed off that there were no pull-ups last Thursday." I tell her that she did an excellent job of teaching me that lesson and I assure her that "If there aren't any pull-ups tomorrow, I'm gonna pull-up a dozen guys whether they've done anything or not, cause I'm treacherous like that."

One of the comps stands to address me—probably to ask me to curb my aggression—but Dr. Smith instructs him to sit down. "Are you finished, Mr. Cox?"

"No," I reply. "Your little temper tantrum didn't teach me anything. All you did was humiliate me and everyone in this room, just to prove to us that you're in charge. Just because you're angry—"

"I'm not angry!" she snaps. "I'm not angry! *You* don't have the power to make me angry, you don't have . . ." He words trail off, but it's too late. Everyone in the room could see she was a fraction of a second from losing control. The Doctor pulls herself together and with a sneer she asks, "Is there anything else, Mr. Cox?"

"You know what, I could go on and on about what a useless exercise in power-orientation that was. Super optimism . . . resentment . . . but I'm so desperate to get outta this room, I'm willing to say you were absolutely right to have us sit here for three day—"

"But you don't believe that do you?"

I ignore the question and retort, "I've *never* wanted a Xanax more than I do at this very moment."

Directly after the meeting, Dr. Smith calls my process DTS, Mrs. Garcia, and Anderson, my content DTS, into her office; wherein she grumbles that they had both reported that I had been making progress. "What the hell was that?" she snaps. "He just challenged me in front of the entire community."

"He's frustrated," replies Anderson. "He's getting better."

Throughout the day, a minimum of thirty of my peers make various comments like "You're my idol" and "You're a fucking legend, Cox." So, I'm feeling pretty good when, at three o'clock, Anderson stops me in the hallway. "What were you thinking?" she asks. "Dr. Smith is furious. You've gotta apologize."

"I'm not apologizing. I gave her a little shot of humility." I push an imaginary plunger into a syringe with my thumb, middle and ring fingers, and I chuckle. "Everyone needs a shot of humility, every once in a while—"

"Not her Cox, not *her!*" Anderson snaps back. "Don't you want to graduate?"

I give a noncommittal shrug and grunt, "I'm indifferent."

The following morning, two dozen inmates raise their hands when asked about possible pull-ups.

WHEN EDDIE HOLLOWAY says, "I wanna pull-up Miss Martin," I damn near fall out of my chair. Princess is the golden child of the program. I can't imagine she's done anything wrong. However, Holloway, who is roughly 30 pounds overweight, explains that Miss Martin had approached him the previous day and asked if she could keep a *Men's Health* magazine she'd borrowed. When he told her no, "Miss Martin, said, 'Why, it ain't like you read them. As chunky as you are, you're gonna be payin' for *pussy* for the rest of your life.'"

Half the community has to suppress their laughter. Hell, one of the DTS's has to walk out of the room.

Holloway went on to explain that Miss Martin was struggling with "caring" and he gave her an intervention. Then, two other peers stand and give feedback on the incident.

A day or two later, a drug dealer named Robert Elie, pulls-up Major. Major is a huge flamboyant gay oxy dealer from the Florida Keys. Understand, Major's job is passing out sports gear in the equipment area of the recreation yard.

"Man," says Elie, "I was on the rec yard on Tuesday and you was like, 'Yo, you forgot to turn in the ab-roller-thingy.' I was like 'My bad, bro.' But then you said, 'I could pull you up for cognitive indolence, but I ain't gonna do that, so, like just buy me a couple of bags of chips and we're all good.'" Everyone's jaw drops. The room goes totally silent. We're talking crickets. Elie explains that he initially had thought it was a joke, but then Major reminded him not to forget the chips. "So, you suffering from power orientation and, and, and I want you to know..." Elie points, almost aggressively, at Major and barks, "I ain't gotcha *fuckin'* chips man!"

I laugh. Several of the surrounding participants shush me, but I don't care. *This shit is fucking hilarious.* I tell myself, *This has got to go into the book.*

MISS MARTIN WILL NOT STOP PUSHING me to finish my treatment plan. It's due soon and unlike my last stint in the program, I have to turn in something. I'm tempted to turn in nothing and see what happens, however, Princess is unwilling to let this happen.

"No," she says, "Doc'll kick you out." My tranny cellie is insisting that I finish all of the assignments that make up my treatment plan.

"Fuck that," I grumble. "I'm leaving."

"Unh uh, *Boo!*" snaps Miss Martin, in a spot on imitation of a ghetto fabulous black girl. "You gonna stop with all that leaving me talk."

This makes me laugh. Several guys stop in front of our cell to observe Princes snapping her fingers and shifting her head.

"Come on," I say, "cut the gangster shit; I know you were raised middle-class." In fact, she was on her high school golf team. "You were a member of the country club. You're practically a white girl... You're Taylor Swift."

This makes Miss Martin furious and she barks, "Oh no you didn't!" She then starts giving me a hard time about dropping out of the program and insists that I need the counselling.

There are at least six guys now standing at the opening to our cell, listening to us hurl comical insults at one another. Which isn't good for me. I ask her several times to drop the subject, but she digs in.

Finally, in an effort to get Miss Martin off the subject, I ask, "What're you so pissed off about?" I feign concern and add, "Is this because you're gaining weight?"

She rears back in horror and gasps, "Ohmigod, am I?!" and rushes into the bathroom to check herself out in the mirror.

The comment sends her into such a tailspin that the following day she starts a *The Biggest Loser* weight loss contest in the unit as an extra credit project.

DTS ANDERSON STOPS ME as I'm walking out of my content class. She wants to know if I've apologized to Dr. Smith yet. "You were serious about that?" I ask, feigning confusion. "I thought—"

"Cox," she growls, "don't con me." She tells me it's important to keep The Doctor on my side. "She likes you, and, whether you believe it or not, you're gonna need that in the next phase."

I've actually enjoyed the fact that Dr. Smith is irritated with me. The random private therapy sessions have ceased and the box is firmly rooted on the shelf. But Anderson has gone pretty easy on me and I'd like to keep it that way. More importantly, for some unexplainable reason, I like her.

Both Tamayo and one of the orderlies are seated in Dr. Smith's office when I enter. They're going over the upcoming bed rotation. The Doctor glances up and I can see she's masking annoyance. "Cox," she says. Then grins and asks, "How's your ass?"

The comment takes me off guard and I reply, "It's still a little sore; how's yours." It just came out and I instantly regretted it.

Her face becomes flush and she scoffs. Tamayo and the orderly immediately avert their eyes. "So," she says, "you said I embarrassed you. I mean I could see if I'd had you stripped down naked and made you stand in the middle of the morning meeting, sure you'd be embarrassed, but all I did was ask you to sit in a chair... or maybe you're into that. I don't know."

I want to tell her that she's justifying her actions—exhibiting super optimism and power orientation—but I don't. I know Dr. Smith wants to tear me a new asshole and she's smart and cunning enough to do it. "Yes, ma'am," I grunt. She stares at me expectantly and I force an act of contrition. "I just wanted to apologize."

She doesn't acknowledge my regret. Instead, she waves her hand dismissively and says, "You can go Cox."

An hour later, I stop Hammette as he's exiting his office. I ask about the management variable and he informs me that the Bureau has yet to place the hold on me. "Fuck!" I gasp. "I need it," I glance in the direction of Dr. Smith's office and add, "I've had a couple close calls."

"I've heard." Hammette grins and confides in me, "You know she's pissed, right? What were you thinking?"

ATTITUDE CHECK

SATURDAY, AUGUST 10, 2018, my cellie's crazy hormonal ass kept giving me a hard time about not working on my treatment plan. "Why is this chick bugging me about something that's none of her business?! Fucking overachiever Super-Dapper!" It got so bad that she's actually threatened to pull me up!

Which attitude was I struggling with-Humility.

After thinking about it, I realized that my cellie was only trying to help. She only wants the best for me.

Which attitude was I demonstrating-Open mindedness.

If I continue with these positive attitudes I will be able to deal with the stress that comes from busy-body know-it-alls.

DR. SMITH WANTS ME TO STOP SPEAKING to Pete. Much like the upper echelon of The Church of Scientology, Dr. Smith thinks RDAP participants shouldn't associate with anyone that isn't engrossed in treatment. They're considered "negative" influences.

Scientology is a blend of psychology and spirituality. The core belief is that all humans contain an immortal spirit and by improving that spirit members can meet their full potential. However, within Scientology there is a strong push to disassociate members from nonmembers.

"I just think your time would be better spent with guys from the community," she says. "Like minded individuals."

"No!" I retort. "He's the most positive person I know." I tell her that Pete once told me that you can't come to prison, continue to behave in the same manner that led you to prison, and expect to get out and not return. That one statement resonated with me and helped reshape the way I think. Furthermore, I bounce ideas off him and he edits every true crime I write. "I'm not gonna stop talking to him."

She huffs in frustration, "You're refusing?"

"I'm refusing." She's adamant, but I won't budge. I try to

explain that the writing is therapy for me. It gives me purpose. "It gives my life meaning."

She scoffs this time, and says, "You know how I feel about the urban novels."

The blinds to the office are closed and it's dark. She's got the whole Morticia Adams thing going on today. "You know," I say, "It wouldn't kill you to let in some natural light."

She ignores the suggestion and asks about my log. She wants to know if I'm still documenting the time I spend on the computer and I tell her I am. "Cox, seriously, if I asked you to go get the log right now, could you?"

"Is this really what you called me in here for?" I haven't written anything in the log in weeks. I stand and say, "I'll go get it right now—"

"No!" she snaps. "Sit down. You're not going anywhere." I remain standing—I'm dying to get out of the office. She points to the chair and says, "Now." I sit and she asks how the letters to my son are progressing. "Have you noticed an improvement?"

I can't get through a single letter without tearing up, but I don't address it. I can picture the box and I mentally press down on the lid. "You're not going to fix me Dr. Smith," I reply. "All the king's horses and all the king's men . . ."

Chapter Twelve

"I have never seen battles quite as terrifyingly beautiful as the ones I fight when my mind splinters and races, to swallow me into my own madness, again."—Nicole Lyons

JAVONISE, MISS MARTIN'S EX-BOYFRIEND, refuses to speak to her. He is preparing to leave for the halfway house, as such, he is distancing himself. She spent Saturday moping around the unit.

Sunday morning, I notice she's crying and it's obvious she wants someone to talk to. Unfortunately, I'm that guy.

I sit opposite her on my bed as she goes into what a crushing blow Javonise's recent behavior has been. "I can't stop thinking about how much time I wasted thinking we would be together on the street," she wipes away some tears and sniffles back the congestion running down her nose. "I know you're gonna say I'm too good for him, but it hurts."

"You're too good for him."

Miss Martin smiles. "It still hurts."

"You don't get to choose who you fall in love with."

This sends her into a full blown crying spree. I want to console Miss Martin and I almost pat her on the knee—as a sign of support. However, due to the Bureau's refusal to pay for the "corrective surgery" Miss Martin is still trapped inside a six-foot tall black man's body, and, based on my knowledge of the African male anatomy, she most likely has two inches of dick on me. Therefore, I resist the act of compassion.

HAMMETTE INFORMS ME that the BOP has placed a management variable on me. "Are you gonna sign out?" he asks. "Before you get yourself tossed?"

"Maybe," I reply. The drug program's housing unit is *much* nicer than my old housing unit—B-4 is a shithole! Plus, this unit has multiple microwaves and the inmates are much politer. By the end of the month I should receive a date for my release to the halfway house in Tampa, Florida. "I might hangout until the date comes back."

Because I'm within weeks of dropping out of RDAP, I no longer to pretend to be participating in the program. As a result, I stop participating in both my content and process groups and the morning meetings.

GUERRIERO AND I are standing in line in the cafeteria. It's Saturday, August 11, 2018, and a couple of Cuban RDAP participants—an obnoxious wannabe gangster named Christopher Castillo and Jose Battle,* a new peer with a chip on his shoulder—are arguing in front of us.

* Name has been changed.

I'm not really paying attention; however, I am staring in their general direction when Battle catches my eye and says, "What's up; you gotta problem?"

He clearly thinks I'm eavesdropping, but I honestly couldn't tell you what they were discussing. Both Battle and Castillo turn toward us. Then, suddenly, Castillo barks, "Yeah, what *are* you lookin' at?"

I don't respond to either of them. Instead, I turn to Guerriero and grin at what idiots the two wannabe thugs are. I'm not the least bit concerned about either of them.

Castillo throws his chest out and begins mouthing off—something about me being an arrogant prick—but it's Battle that says, "What the fuck are you looking at? What, do I have a dick on my fuckin' head or somethin'?!" This makes me smile, which only pisses off the two wannabe thugs even more.

Understand, I still haven't said one word. At this point, Guerriero steps in between us. He tells them to back off. Several other peers step between us and the confrontation is defused. However, the following day, I'm walking down the hallway and Castillo steps in front of me and thrusts his outstretched hand at me.

"Sorry, man," he says. "I wanna apologize for yesterday."

The most likely reason for the apology is Castillo's fear that I might put him or his friend up. I don't say a thing to him. I just scoff and keep walking.

Guerriero insists that Castillo is going to pull me up for holding resentment or refusing to confront and level. "Arrogance, he could get you on anything."

The next morning, when the facilitator asks if there are any pull-ups, Castillo raises his hand. He's two rows behind me and I know he's going to address me. Sure enough, standing in the midst of the crowded room, Castillo says, "I wanna pull-up Mr. Cox."

Keep in mind, RDAP protocol states that if a participant is pulled-up, even on fabricated or manipulated information, the inmate must allow the pull-up and stick with the format. He can later appeal the inaccuracy of the pull-up to his DTS. Regardless of the rules, on numerous occasions I have informed members of the program, as well as the DTS's, that if I were *ever* addressed on some fabricated bullshit, despite policy, they should expect me to have a Chernobyl-size-meltdown on the guy conducting the pull-up. Damn the consequences.

The moment I turn to see Castillo I'm instantly enraged, and it's obvious. My face hardens and my body tenses. Guys seated near me whisper for me to calm down. Stick to the protocol.

Unexpectedly, DTS DeMille steps out of the room.

I listen patiently as Castillo twists the scene in the cafeteria. Unambiguously, he states that I made several cracks at his expense, thereby escalating the confrontation. *Lying sack of shit,* I think. *When it's time for me to summarize, I'm taking this guy's head off.* I remain patient and say nothing. To Castillo's credit, he does portray the scene in the hallway accurately.

I turn to DTS Anderson, clinch my jaw and squeeze my eyelids slightly. It's clear that I'm about to snap. She pumps her open hand slightly—signaling for me to calm down—and I turn back to Castillo.

He then begins to tell me that I was eavesdropping and that I suffer from caring and resentment. At this point, Dr. Smith walks into the room.

The facilitator calls on two peers to give feedback. As they stand Dr. Smith say, "Cox, are you okay?" I don't answer, but I turn toward her and she can see the rage written all over my face. "I need clarity." Dr. Smith asks the group. "Who else was in the cafeteria?"

Guerriero stands. He admits that he wasn't in the hallway with us, however, he explains that during the confrontation in the cafeteria I'd never said one word to Castillo or Battle. Two more peers stand and backup Guerriero's account.

The Doctor can see I'm still irritated. "The one thing I know about Mr. Cox," she says to the community, "is he's unabashedly honest; at times to a fault." The Doctor turns to me and asks, "Cox, why didn't you shake Mr. Castillo's hand in the hallway?"

"Resentment," I admit. In my opinion, Castillo was only apologizing to try and quash a possible reprisal. "The pull-up was damage control."

"I agree," says Dr. Smith. She tells the community that I had every right to be angry with Castillo and Battle for their behavior and that she didn't see an issue with me holding resentment toward them. This, of course, is completely contrary to multiple speeches she'd given us in the past. Dr. Smith instructs Castillo and I to take our seats and says, "I'm shutting the pull-up down."

"JESUS CHRIST COX," laughs Padula, "are you fuckin' that bitch?"

"Don't do that bro," I reply. "That's how rumors get started. Don't even joke about it." Padula, Guerriero, and I are in the library. I was in the middle of writing when they ambushed me. "She just saw that it was a bullshit pull-up and—"

"No!" interrupts Paduala, "something's up. You're in her

office all of the time. Then you two have a fight in the middle of the morning meeting—"

"It was a disagreement."

"Then, she protects you from what looked like a solid pull-up, to me."

"It wasn't a solid pull-up!" I growl. I point at Guerriero and say, "He can vouch for that, and as far as her calling me into her office, trust me, I'd happily never step into that office again. Every time I go in there I end up crying like a small child." In fact, I've become so conditioned by the negative experiences, I now having a Pavlovian response when I hear Dr. Smith request my presence. "I actually tear up as I'm approaching the office; that's how bad it is."

"Oh shit," says Guerriero.

"That's what I'm saying," I snap. "I've gotta get outta that unit."

ATTITUDE CHECK

WEDNESDAY, AUGUST 15, 2018, I needed to use the phone to call my mom, but they weren't working. It's always something with this fucking place! How hard is it to keep the phones working?

Which attitude was I struggling with- Gratitude.

After thinking about it, I realized that the phones are a privilege, not a right. I'm lucky to have them at all. I'll be patient and call later.

Which attitude was I demonstrating- Gratitude.

If I continue to practicing these positive attitudes I will be a much happier person.

ALL OF THE DTS'S ARE SEATED in the darkness of The Doctor's office. Most are singing my praises, with the exception of DeMille —she's noticed that I've stopped participating in the morning meeting and she's not happy about it.

My Big Brother, Neal Taylor, a chunky baldheaded black guy, tries to defend me by saying that I've been working through issues with my son, but DeMille doesn't want to hear this.

"Mr. Cox, you're shutting down," she says. "Are you hearing what we're saying? Don't you want to graduate and get the year off?"

Before I can respond, Dr. Smith interjects, "He doesn't have enough time to get the full year off, and the little bit of time Mr. Cox might get... he doesn't want."

I glance at her. We have never discussed the matter, yet she somehow knows I'm not in the program for the time, but I say nothing.

"Well," snaps DeMille in a huff, "the third phase is coming up and we're going to expect you to step it up and be one of the leaders in the community."

I have to stop myself from laughing. If asked, I couldn't even reciting the philosophy.

AS SOON AS I BEGIN TYPING Dr. Smith calls me into her office. I let her know that I'm in the middle of something, regardless, she points at the chair and asks, "Have you reached out to your son?"

"No," I respond. "I've done everything possible to connect with him, but he just doesn't want a relationship." I'd drawn pictures for him, written letters, and emails. I'd even tried to get him to talk to me on the phone. "I tried to convince my ex-wife to bring him here to see me—"

"What'd she say?"

"She said she had no intentions of dragging her son to a prison." Dr. Smith appears irritated by my answer—clearly disappointed that my ex-wife wouldn't force my son to visit his father. "Look, she made the best decision she could at the time. She's not wrong. Everything that has happened, I had coming. It's no one's fault but my own."

"Do you still love her?"

My eyes fill with tears at the thought of Keyla and Cassio, and all she'd done to make sure that he stays a part of my family's life. All she must have had to endure because of my absence. "I'll always love her," I mutter. "How could I not."

ATTITUDE CHECK

SATURDAY, AUGUST 18, 2018, my crazy hormonal cellie decided to stop talking to me, as well as most of her peers, for some 12-year-old girlish reason. It irritates me to the point that I'm seriously considering tying her dreadlocks to the bed post while she naps.

Which attitude was I struggling with- Humility.

After thinking about it, I realize that I should be thankful that I'm not going through what ever mood swings this chick is going through. Plus, it's not like I couldn't use the break from listening to her bitch and moan about her ex-boyfriend.

Which attitude was I demonstrating- Gratitude.

If I continue to work on these positive attitudes I will be a more patient person that is able to handle the stress that accompanies moody six-foot tall trannys.

THE DOCTOR IS STARING AT ME. She wants to discuss my son. "I don't wanna talk about him," I reply. "There's no reason for me to talk about him Dr. Smith, he's gone."

"You don't know that," she retorts. She tells me that my son is young and stubborn, but, as he matures he'll come to understand that everyone makes mistakes and, eventually, he'll want to get to know who his father is. "At some point, he'll want to have a conversation with you Cox; don't you want to be able to have that conversation without becoming emotional?"

I hunch over at the thought of weeping in front of my son and I whisper, "I don't wanna talk about this anymore." The room is stifling and all I can think about is escaping. "He's never going to forgive me. I don't deserve it."

"Even if he doesn't," she replies in a soft tone, "you need to forgive yourself."

DTS ANDERSON GLARES AT ME from the corner of the room. The facilitator just asked if anyone wants to volunteer for the word of the day. She wants me to participate, to stand and be present in the meeting. To articulate what the word of the day means to me. There are fifty hands in the air, but mine isn't among them.

Yesterday, Hammette gave me my halfway house date. I will be leaving the first part of January 2019. There is very little chance the Bureau will ship me to a camp for four months.

Directly after the morning meeting I scribble out a quick note to Dr. Smith. Specifically, I'm requesting to be removed from the program and transferred out of the unit. Hammette has already agreed to have me moved to the C-1 Housing Unit.

Two hours later, I ask Tamayo if he'll grab a phase one, two, and three colored band from Dr. Smith's stash. I explain that my plan is to photograph the bands for the jacket cover. "For the book."

He grins at me and asks, "You don't want all of them? I can get you all of them."

"No, I only need the first three phases." I'd gone straight into the program both times, so, I never received a yellow wait band, and, although I wasn't going to complete phase three, I had started the phase. "I just need the phases. I'm not gonna graduate."

Chapter Thirteen

"When people leave cults, they don't know that they left a cult."—Sean Durkin

I'D LIKE TO SAY IT WAS AUGUST 20, 2018, but I can't be one hundred percent sure, regardless, Dr. Smith asks me to reconsider dropping out. "You're doing so good, Cox. Don't do this," she pleas. "You can still get three months off your sentence."

"Yeah," I say, "but we both know that if things don't go right for me, there's a good chance I'll be coming back here. I'll be in my fifties and I'll need the whole year."

Dr. Smith shakes her head. "I wish you wouldn't say things like that."

"Plus, you're assuming I'm gonna pass phase three, but, for someone like me . . . it's the hardest phase." It's the only phase that would give me a significant problem and she knows that. There would be open discussions in both my content and process groups concerning the failed relationships with my son and father as well as the letter from my ex-wife. "No thanks," I chuckle. "I'll do the extra three months."

MY FRP PAYMENT is due, so, I transfer all of my money out of my inmate account. I do this by purchasing computer and phone minutes. This drains my account to nearly zero. Specifically, I do this so that when the payment hits the following day, it will bounce. However, a friend on the street ends up sending me money and it hits my account just before my FRP does. As a result, I end up making my FRP payment.

I am furious about this.

Over dinner that night Pete tells me to stop bitching about it. "You're going to have to get used to paying toward restitution on the street. You're P.O. (probation officer) is never going to put up with your shenanigans."

"I know, Pete," I grumble, "I know."

IT IS MID-DECEMBER AND I HAVE managed to get myself moved to the C-1 Unit. It's a cleaner and more organized unit. Most of the prisoners that populate the unit are either leaving, just graduated RDAP or are waiting to go to RDAP. Unfortunately, the move means that my new counselor will be Counselor Thompson, the redneck that thinks I should be paying one hundred dollars a month in FRP.

I'm in the process of mailing some of my clothes home. Although I've asked Counselor Thompson several times, he is so ineffective that he cannot manage to pick up a couple of large boxes from Receiving & Departure so that I can mail my stuff home. His incompetence causes me to have to make my own boxes.

Once I've filled out the paperwork—this is also a part of his job—I knock on his office door and wait in the hallway to be called. He has to sign off on the shipping document and bring it to the Receiving & Departure clerk. I can hear Counselor Thompson and Counselor Hammette talking shit in the office. Some lieutenant got a DUI and a correctional officer is hooked on oxycodone. *This place is a fucking soap opera.*

Eventually he calls me into the office and I hand him the paperwork. The form has multiple carbon copies, each one is a different color. He signs the paperwork and tells me to take my copy.

"Which one's mine," I ask, flipping through the copies.

He shakes his head as if I'm a dunce. Then he slowly flips through the pages and points to a tiny font in the lower left hand corner of the form and says, "Yellow Inmate Copy. You see that Cox?" He glances at Hammette with a half-grin and addresses me as if I were a child, "You see where is says Yellow Inmate Copy? That's your copy; you're the inmate."

I immediately laugh at the absurdity of his contempt and Hammette asks, "What is so funny?"

"I was just thinking about time," I reply with a chuckle, "a month from now this conversation would go vastly different, but at this moment I have to take it."

Hammette laughs at this, but Thompson seems annoyed. He thrusts the yellow copy at me and grunts, "We're done here Cox."

THE NIGHT BEFORE I LEAVE Pete and I walk the compound. Guys are wishing me luck and telling me to stay out of trouble. Just before the compound officer announces the compound is closed, Pete tells me not to lose focus. "Stick to the plan. Keep your head down and overhead low. Build the website and push the stories."

I'd already reached out to a few reporters about my personal journey from infamous con man to true crime writer. Everyone finds the story compelling. "I know what I'm supposed to do," I say. "I'm gonna push it."

"Netflix, Hulu, Apple . . . they're all looking for these types of stories."

"I know Pete." I take several deep breaths. I try to tell Pete what his friendship has meant to me, but he refuses to listen.

"Don't lose focus. Stick to the plan." His eyes well with tears. Pete says, "Don't come back here," and he abruptly walks away.

THE CORRECTIONAL OFFICER inventorying my property in the Receiving & Departure office is being a dick. It's January 9, 2019, around 9:00 a.m. I have a dozen boxes of legal work as well as the outlines to several stories—including the story you're reading—and three plastic bags of clothing—stuff I'm going to need in the halfway house. "You're gonna have to carry all that shit," says the officer. "I ain't helpin' you with it."

"Well," I mumble, staring at my stuff, "you gotta dolly or a cart?" He tells me he can't give me either and I shrug. "I'll have to make two trips."

"Not gonna happen. Once you leave the facility you can't re-enter the building." He stares at me with a blank expression.

"I'm not leaving without my legal work and clothes," I declare. Unmoved by my dilemma, he just stares. "Well, I guess I'll be staying then..."

"Yeah," he grunts, "that's fine with me. I'll put you in the SHU."

What a lazy fucking prick this guy is, I think. *Fucking waste of a human being.* "I don't give a shit, I'm not leaving without my stuff."

We stare at one another for several seconds and he grunts, "I'll get you a cart."

My brother meets me at the curb, along with my mother and sister-in-law. I sit in the back of the sedan with my mom. She can't stop smiling at me. I know she never thought she'd see me walk out of prison. She holds my hand as we exit the Coleman Complex.

I'm feeling pretty good until my brother says, "I'll bet you're glad to put that place behind you." Abruptly, Pete, Donovan, and half a dozen other guys' faces flash into my mind; an overwhelming sensation of loss washes over me like a warm tide. I'm suddenly in need of oxygen and then, tears fill my eyes.

The feeling of loss is indescribable. I know I should be excited to leave this place; instead, I'm caught somewhere between panic and desperation.

I'd love to tell you that I'm strong and I fight back the tears, but it's simply not true. I cry like a small child for twenty minutes. No one speaks. I guess they're too uncomfortable to say anything or maybe they don't notice.

I long to see my friends.

Chapter Fourteen

"Even if you are on the right track, you'll get run over if you just sit there."—Will Rogers

I PLACE CESAR'S WATCH in the cardboard FedEx envelope and seal the lip. Once I hand it to the clerk at the counter, I text Cesar a photo of the tracking number and call his cell. "It's in the mail."

"What are you going to do now?" he asks. I tell him I still have a few more months in the halfway house and he cuts me off. "For money, Matt; what're you going to do for money?"

"I've got a job and I'm saving my money," I say. "Eventually, I'll have enough to design a website to feature the stories and then, I'll start pitching them." I've resolved myself to the fact that I can't do anything while in the halfway house—there's no Wi-Fi and the inmates aren't allowed to have a computer. "I'll have to wait."

Cesar is worried about me. Specifically, he's worried because I told him that my entire wardrobe consists of three hundred dollars of clothes that I'd bought at Walmart. I'm thrilled with my Walmart clothes, but Cesar is upset. He FedEx's me a box of clothes, everything from Dolce & Gabbana to Calvin Klein. The kind of stuff I can't afford.

During a phone call with Pete, he tells me he doesn't like my plan to wait to build the website. "How much do you need for the website?"

"I don't know," I admit. "I don't even have a laptop." I explain that I could get a used MacBook Pro for around $400. However, I also need Photoshop, an iPhone, a WordPress site and on and on. "There's a bunch of other stuff, like a security certificate, analytics, and—"

"Okay!" snaps Pete. "I'm going to have someone send you the money."

"Who?" I seriously doubt Pete has several thousand dollars to send me.

"Every time I walk across the compound someone stops and asks me how you're doing and if you need anything." They ask him if I've started the website or begun pitching the stories. Pete informs me that he's been telling everyone that I'm fine and that I don't need anything. "From now on," he says, "I'm going to start passing out a list."

"Pete, I can't pay these guys back—"

"No one's asking."

Within two weeks, I receive two used MacBook Pros and roughly three hundred dollars. Within three weeks the amount swells to nearly two thousand dollars. *Fucking amazing!* I can't help but think every time another check arrives.

I cannot begin to tell you how overwhelmingly grateful I am to Pete and the guys at Coleman for pooling their limited resources to help further my agenda.

Because I'm not allowed to have a laptop in the halfway house, it takes me three months to design my website: Inside True Crime; as well as the jacket covers to the true crime stories, illustrations, and the photo lineups that populate the site.

THE AUGUST ISSUE OF *THE ATLANTIC* and *Forbes* magazine come out in late-July. Both feature articles covering my story as a con man turned true crime author. Hoping to garner some positive publicity, I'd reached out to the reporters several months before I was released.

The pieces not only plunged into my metamorphosis, but also explore several of my subjects' stories. Specifically, Rachel Monroe with *The Atlantic* wrote, "*Cox's services were in demand enough that he had his pick of subjects. He wasn't particularly interested in telling a drug saga . . . The business tycoon who at-*

tempted to build the world's largest private militia? Sure, he could work with that. The prison lawyer who accidentally uncovered a botched cartel assassination? That was a story he wanted to tell."

The *Forbes* article, by Walter Pavlo, stated, "*Cox's plan while lying on the cot in his cell was to get out of prison, create his own website—focusing specifically on true crime... He launched the site, Inside True Crime, upon his release from prison in July. 'Anyone can read the articles,' he tells me, 'there are pictures of the subject and illustrations. I just wanted it to be fun but I'm hoping that this is the start of my new life. Cox has already uploaded nearly twenty stories on Inside True Crime; everything from tales of international narco traffickers to confidence men. One of Cox's personal favorites is Bent, the tale of a homeless teen turned credit card counterfeiter who disappeared with millions of dollars in funds confiscated by the U.S. Secret Service. 'I don't know why,' laughs Cox, 'but I see Justin Bieber playing the stories protagonist, John Boseak.'*"

I am thrilled with the articles. Within weeks, I begin getting emails from multiple production companies in New York and Los Angeles.

It's around 8:45 a.m. on September 23, 2019, I'm seated at a restaurant in the Proper—a boutique hotel located in downtown San Francisco, California. The waitress places my bagel and lox on the table. The plate is warm.

I'm in San Francisco to conduct interviews related to a biography I've been hired to write. It's a vanity project for a renowned attorney with a slew of high profile wins under his belt. An amazing underdog story that I can't wait to dig into.

I check my email while eating my bagel. There's a message from Pete. Within it, he explains that several inmates at the prison subscribe to *The Atlantic*, and, the magazine is being passed around the compound. More interesting, however, is the fact that Dr. Smith has read the article and, according to multiple RDAP participants, The Doctor is furious with me. Specifically, she insists that because I'd written about Joseph Vitale and several events that had occurred during the program, I've violated RDAP's confidentiality.

One of the program inmates tells Pete, "If Cox violates his supervised release, he'd better hope the Bureau doesn't send him back here. Dr. Smith will have him thrown in the hole."

This makes me laugh.

I WOULD LOVE TO REPORT that I'm living in a trendy condo located within a high-rise in downtown Tampa, Florida, but I'm not. Currently, I'm renting a spare room from a family that lives in a massive house on a lake and I drive a piece of shit Jeep—the air conditioning doesn't work and it burns oil like retreating Iraqi soldiers.

I have what can best be described as a contentious relationship with my probation officer. My monthly restitution payments are a constant source of strife; nor is she thrilled with the fact that I'm continuously traveling.

Moreover, my supervision requires me to participate in a three month long behavior modification group therapy course. However, during the initial "get to know you" session with the therapist, I made the mistake of telling her that if things didn't come together for me, I had every intention of committing a massive fraud.

In retrospect this was a bad idea. Specifically, because the therapist disclosed the confession to my probation officer. Consequently, she waived the limited group sessions. Instead, I'm now required to attend one-on-one individual sessions with a therapist once per week for the duration of my probation or until I show marked improvement. *Unfuckingbelievable!*

It hasn't been a perfect transition, but I'm doing better than I had expected. When I begin to feel too self-assured, too arrogant, too cocky, I tell myself, *Be humble. Be thankful. Don't forget you're supposed to be in prison right now.*

On the upside, I see my mother four to five times a week. We take long walks and eat breakfast together. She loves to pick at me about needing a haircut and not shaving regularly. I have never been happier, notwithstanding, I miss the guys at Coleman every single day. As crazy as this sounds, there are times I am desperate to go back. It's a completely irrational feeling that I can't explain.

Epilogue

LUIS MUNOZ MARIN INTERNATIONAL AIRPORT in San Juan, Puerto Rico, is a little chillier than I'd expected. It's 7:30 a.m. on Thursday, January 23, 2020, and I'm about to board my plane. I spent the previous night having dinner and drinks with a producer who's had several series on Netflix—she's in San Juan shooting some movie with Alec Baldwin. She wanted to discuss a possible series regarding one or two of the stories. We're supposed to talk next week.

I'm sipping a Starbucks coffee, standing at the terminal watching the travelers waddle by with their carry-ons. Planes are lifting off in the distance. *I still can't believe I'm free,* I think. *It's surreal.*

My cell rings as I toss the empty cup into a trash receptacle. It's Davy Rothbart, a journalist for *GQ* magazine. He's also a screenwriter, independent documentary producer, and director. Davy's been helping me navigate the entertainment industry. Over the last several months he's pitched the idea of a streaming series based on my life to multiple production companies in LA. Davy tells me that a meeting we'd had days earlier with a producer and some executive went well. "They wanna work out an agreement to do the series. I've got an agent with UTA (United Talent Agency) that wants to represent you in the negotiations."

"How serious are they?" I ask. The woman working the Southwest gate announces passengers may begin boarding the plane.

"I wouldn't be surprised if, by this time next year, you don't have a series on Netflix or Hulu."

Unfuckingbelievable! I tell myself. *This has gotta go in the book.*

About the Author

MATTHEW B. COX is the author of *Once a Gunrunner, Bailout, Generation Oxy, Bent,* and *Shark in the Housing Pool.*

He is a graduate of the University of South Florida, he lives and works in Central Florida.